Fairbanks

ALASKA GEOGRAPHIC®

Volume 22, Number 1

The Alaska Geographic Society

To teach many more to better know and more wisely use our natural resources

Editor
Penny Rennick

Production Director
Kathy Doogan

Staff Writer
L.J. Campbell

Bookkeeper/Database Manager
Vickie Staples

Marketing Manager
Pattey Parker

Board of Directors
Richard Carlson
Kathy Doogan
Penny Rennick

Robert A. Henning, *President Emeritus*

Postmaster: Send address changes to
ALASKA GEOGRAPHIC®
P.O. Box 93370
Anchorage, Alaska 99509-3370

PRINTED IN U.S.A.

ISBN: 1-56661-025-7

Price to non-members this issue: $19.95

COVER: *Minus temperatures are common in Fairbanks in winter. (Craig Brandt)*

PREVIOUS PAGE: *A statue of the First Family adorns this fountain in a plaza overlooking the Chena River in downtown Fairbanks. (Harry M. Walker)*

FACING PAGE: *Horacio Lombardi wins the Felix Pedro look-a-like contest. Pedro's gold discovery assured the survival of the trading post on the Chena. (Steven Seiller)*

ALASKA GEOGRAPHIC® is published quarterly by The Alaska Geographic Society, 639 West International Airport Road, Unit 38, Anchorage, AK 99518. Second-class postage paid at Anchorage, Alaska, and additional mailing offices. Copyright © 1995 by The Alaska Geographic Society. All rights reserved. Registered trademark: Alaska Geographic, ISSN 0361-1353; Key title Alaska Geographic.

THE ALASKA GEOGRAPHIC SOCIETY is a non-profit, educational organization dedicated to improving geographic understanding of Alaska and the North, putting geography back in the classroom and exploring new methods of teaching and learning.

SOCIETY MEMBERS receive *ALASKA GEOGRAPHIC®*, a quality publication that devotes each quarterly issue to monographic in-depth coverage of a northern geographic region or resource-oriented subject.

MEMBERSHIP in The Alaska Geographic Society costs $39 per year, $49 to non-U.S. addresses. ($31.20 of the membership fee is for a one-year subscription to *ALASKA GEOGRAPHIC®*.) Order from The Alaska Geographic Society, Box 93370, Anchorage, AK 99509-3370; phone (907) 562-0164, fax (907) 562-0479.

SUBMITTING PHOTOGRAPHS: Please write for a list of upcoming topics or other specific photo needs and a copy of our editorial guidelines. We cannot be responsible for unsolicited submissions. Submissions not accompanied by sufficient postage for return by certified mail will be returned by regular mail.

CHANGE OF ADDRESS: The post office does not automatically forward *ALASKA GEOGRAPHIC®* when you move. To ensure continuous service, please notify us six weeks before moving. Send your new address and your membership number or a mailing label from a recent *ALASKA GEOGRAPHIC®* to: The Alaska Geographic Society, Box 93370, Anchorage, AK 99509-3370.

Color Separations:
GRAPHIC CHROMATICS
Printed by:
THE HART PRESS

The Library of Congress has cataloged this serial publication as follows:

Alaska Geographic. v.1-
    [Anchorage, Alaska Geographic Society] 1972-
    v. ill. (part col.). 23 x 31 cm.
    Quarterly
    Official publication of The Alaska Geographic Society.
    Key title: Alaska geographic, ISSN 0361-1353.

    1. Alaska—Description and travel—1959-
    —Periodicals. I. Alaska Geographic Society.

F901.A266   917.98'04'505   72-92087

Library of Congress 75[79112] MARC-S

ABOUT THIS ISSUE: Dermot Cole, columnist and acting managing editor of the *Fairbanks Daily News-Miner*, wrote the historical overview for this issue on Fairbanks. For an account of one of Fairbanks' pioneer families, we turned to Tricia Brown, long-time former resident of Fairbanks and now the managing editor of *Alaska Magazine*. Janice C. Noll, a teacher at North Pole Middle School, contributed the history of North Pole. Free-lance writer Sean Reid prepared the account on the permafrost tunnel, and another free-lancer George Matz wrote about the Alaska Bird Observatory in "Songbirds in Plight," and about the Tanana Valley State Forest. Staff writer L.J. Campbell wrote the "Golden Heart City" section of the text. For reviewing portions of the text, we thank: Dermot Cole; Tom Bundtzen with the Alaska Division of Geological & Geophysical Surveys; Dr. Tom Kinney, associate professor in the civil engineering department, University of Alaska Fairbanks; and Tom Pogson with the Alaska Bird Observatory.

We thank those who granted interviews and shared their version of Fairbanks life, particularly Dr. William R. Wood, Celia Hunter, Ginny Wood, Lynnette Clark, Pat Walsh, Kathleen Carlo, Johne and Skip Binkley, and Cliff Burglin. For their help in providing information, we also thank R.C. Swainbank with the Alaska Division of Economic Development; Erik Hansen, with the Alaska Department of Natural Resources; Neal Fried, Alaska Department of Labor; Dave Lacey, general manager for Dinyee Corp., Stevens Village; Debra Damron, Public Information Officer, University of Alaska Fairbanks; Carole Lay, with the Fairbanks Convention and Visitors Bureau; Mark Gramstad with the Community Research Center, Fairbanks North Star Borough; Linda Douglass, Public Affairs Officer, Fort Wainwright; and Lt. Steve Rickert, Public Affairs Officer, Eielson Air Force Base.

Contents

Fairbanks, Metropolis of the Tanana

By Dermot Cole

Editor's note: *Dermot Cole, a columnist for the* Fairbanks Daily News-Miner, *is a long-time Alaska journalist and historian. He has written two books:* Frank Barr: Bush Pilot in Alaska and the Yukon *(1986) and* Hard Driving: The 1908 Auto Race from New York to Paris *(1991).*

Judge James Wickersham arrived in the new town of Fairbanks by dog team, making the seven-day trip from Circle during the first week of April 1903. As the six dogs topped the last hills north of town, Wickersham and the dog driver handling the

◀ *Downtown Fairbanks looked like many other town centers in the 1960s. Signs proclaiming radio station KFAR and the* Daily News-Miner *share billing on the tallest building at right. (Steve McCutcheon)*

sled enjoyed a magnificent view that extended to the ice-capped Alaska Range.

"Below us, far and wide, lay the glorious valley we had come to help settle. We sped down the long southern slope, through a beautiful forest of silver birch, out upon a flat plain, over a slough, across an island, through a heavy forest of spruce, and, from the north bank of the Chena River, the Metropolis of the Tanana came into view on the opposite shore."

This new metropolis, founded nine months earlier after Felix Pedro's gold discovery, consisted of an assortment of log buildings, a few tents and a small clearing along the river. Wickersham appointed a deputy recorder to register mining claims. And with the assistance of four lawyers and a deputy marshal, he staked a lot for a courthouse and approved plans for a log jail. The town that Wickersham hoped would be "an American

Dawson" was a modest metropolis even to his eye.

"A rough log structure, with spread-eagle wings looked like a disreputable pig sty, but was in fact, Barnette's trading post, the only mercantile establishment in the new camp. A hundred yards up the stream, also facing the river, a half-finished two-story log building without doors or windows bore the home-made sign on a white cloth, 'Fairbanks Hotel.' Two other small log cabins marked, 'Pioneer,' and 'Northern,' made known to miners with wilderness thirst that civilization and its vices were there," according to the account in Wickersham's book *Old Yukon* (1938).

That "civilization and its vices" were present at all along the Chena River was because of a string of coincidences that started with E.T. Barnette, the first man whoever found himself stuck in Fairbanks.

In 1901, Barnette hired a steamboat to take a load of trading goods up the Tanana River to the site of a proposed trading post along the trail from Valdez on Prince William Sound to Eagle on the Yukon River. The *Lavelle Young* was ascending the Chena River, in an attempt to get around a stretch of rapids on the Tanana River, when the riverboat became stuck and could go no farther because of shallow water.

▼ *Everything from sod huts to two-story buildings characterized downtown Fairbanks in 1904. The log building and lean-to at left center were among the first buildings built by Fairbanks' founder, E.T. Barnette. The Northern Commercial Co. store stands at right. (Historical Photograph Collection, Photo no. 66-67-1, Archives, University of Alaska Fairbanks, courtesy of Dermot Cole)*

At 4 p.m. on Aug. 26, 1901, the *Lavelle Young* tied up along the south bank of the Chena River in the heart of what is now downtown Fairbanks to unload Barnette and his $20,000 stockpile of food, clothing and equipment. Barnette had tried to persuade Capt. C.W. Adams to take him several miles downstream to the mouth of the river, but the captain refused. His $6,000 contract with Barnette said that if the *Lavelle Young* could not navigate the river, the freight would be unloaded on its banks. There was a reason for Adams' insistence. Because the riverboat did not have steam winches, traveling downstream with a full load in shallow water would increase the odds of hitting a sandbar and being delayed for several days.

As the riverboat belched smoke and departed, E.T. and Isabelle Barnette made no attempt to disguise their emotions. "Mrs.

Barnette was crying when we left the next day, as it did not look good to her either," Adams recalled in a letter written in 1948. "Capt. Barnette was quite angry with me because I would not take him to the mouth of the Slough, but later that winter I saw him in Dawson on his way outside and he was all smiles and told me that I could not have put him off in a better place."

Barnette's stockpile would have remained on the banks of the Chena only temporarily, but for the second coincidence — the discovery of gold by Felix Pedro the following July about 12 miles from Barnette's cache.

Pedro was an industrious Italian immigrant who became a coal miner, like his father. Pedro worked for several years in French and Italian coal mines before shipping out for the United States in 1883. He never learned to write and he didn't drink or gamble. He worked in coal mines across the

United States before abandoning that life to look for gold in the North.

Pedro was no stranger to hardship and he willingly spent months at a time in the woods, going from valley to valley in search of the precious metal. In 1898, Pedro and a partner were prospecting in the Tanana Hills when they stumbled onto the richest creek either one had ever seen. They were nearly out of food, however, and they marked the creek with a boat and a cache, planning to return. They never found the lost creek again, but Pedro did not stop looking. He discovered a new gold find four years later.

On July 28, 1902, the 42-year-old miner showed up at Barnette's cache and said that he had found gold on a small creek to the north. The stream became Pedro Creek and the hill from which he had seen Barnette's steamboat a year earlier was named Pedro Dome. Pedro "now seems to be sure of fortune's smile," the *Fairbanks Miner* reported later.

The discovery changed everything for Barnette, who recognized right away that this could be the start of a stampede that would bring paying customers. He forgot about moving upstream on the Tanana and decided to stake his claim with a town on the Chena. Barnette became the town's first mayor and its first postmaster. He used his political and business connections to amass a fortune in Alaska during the next decade. But his tenure in Fairbanks would be marked by turmoil and controversy. At various times he was accused of all sorts of underhanded actions including salting a mine, hoarding supplies to

raise food prices and defrauding customers at his bank.

When people in Fairbanks discovered some years later that Barnette, as a 24-year-old, had done time in Oregon in 1887 for larceny and had been banished from the state forever, his reputation was further sullied. He left Alaska in disgrace about a decade after the founding of Fairbanks, with many bank depositors blaming him for the institution's failure.

But all that was in the future when

▲ *Until the railroad connected Fairbanks with the coast in 1923, most commerce in and out of the Interior city went by riverboat on the Chena, Tanana and finally the Yukon rivers. The* Lavelle Young, *Capt. Adams' steamship that had originally deposited E.T. Barnette and his supplies on a wooded bank of the Chena, returns probably about 1904 to the town it helped found. (Charles Bunnell Collection, Photo no. 58-1026-1581, Archives, University of Alaska Fairbanks, courtesy of Dermot Cole)*

▲ *During summers, people and goods could reach Fairbanks on the rivers. But the summers were short, and an overland trail to Circle City on the Yukon River no longer sufficed for the growing town. In 1903, the Senate's Committee on Territories sent representatives to Alaska to assess transportation needs. Alaskans urged the senators to build wagon roads, a message the senators took to heart. Congress formed a Board of Road Commissioners, which in 1906 began construction of a wagon road from Valdez on Prince William Sound to Fairbanks. Horse-drawn stages, such as the one shown here, traversed the trail, carrying passengers, mail and packages. (Steve McCutcheon)*

Barnette spoke at a miners' meeting in September 1902 and persuaded the men to name the camp "Fairbanks." By doing so, Barnette was fulfilling a promise he had made to Wickersham, one of the most powerful men in Alaska. Wickersham first met Barnette when the *Lavelle Young* was headed upstream in 1901. Wickersham was on his way to Nome when the boat he was on, the *Leah*, tied up alongside the *Lavelle Young* at the mouth of the Tanana River.

In a land with no legislature and a governor with few powers, Wickersham's word was law in the 300,000 square miles of the Third Judicial District. Wickersham, 45, was a Republican from Tacoma, Wash. who had been

appointed judge by President William McKinley in 1900. In the years that followed, he became one of the dominant figures in the territory, an early proponent of Alaska statehood and a delegate to Congress for 14 years.

One of Wickersham's mentors, and the man who had helped get him his appointment as a judge was Sen. Charles W. Fairbanks of Indiana. Wickersham asked Barnette to name his trading post after Fairbanks. Knowing the value of having friends in high places, Barnette agreed: "If we should ever want aid at the national capital we would have the friendship of someone who could help us."

In return for this favor from Barnette, Wickersham promised to do whatever he could to help the town succeed. Wickersham made good on the promise when he moved his courthouse to Fairbanks, putting an official stamp of approval on the new town. The courthouse was built on land in downtown Fairbanks donated by Barnette, who had claimed a piece of property 350 feet long and 350 feet wide.

Politics dictated the name of the town, the location of the courthouse and the name of two of its first streets. No one argued with Wickersham's suggestion that two of the main streets in Fairbanks be named after other members of Congress who were allies of Wickersham, Francis Cushman of Tacoma and John Lacey of Iowa.

With the tenuous status that was common to all mining camps, taking steps to win favors in Washington, D.C., was nearly as important as good publicity.

Just after Christmas 1902, Barnette dispatched musher Jurio Wada to Dawson to carry news of the gold strike. The headline, "RICH STRIKE MADE IN THE TANANA" greeted readers of the *Yukon Sun* on Jan. 17, 1903, triggering a midwinter stampede that caused hundreds to head for Fairbanks. The exaggerated account led to trouble later when the stampeders discovered that almost no mining was going on, that the creeks had been tied up by mining speculators and there was no work, no money and a food shortage in Fairbanks. The claims were staked by a few groups of men using power of attorney rights to file claims for others. In this tense atmosphere, Barnette had a dozen armed men standing guard inside his trading post.

"Before there was any bloodshed, the miners' group and Barnette came to an agreement," historian Terrence Cole wrote of this conflict in *Crooked Past*, (1991), a book about early Fairbanks. "The captain agreed to cut the price of his flour in half and also stop forcing the miners to buy canned goods with their flour."

Gold had been discovered, but it would take money and machinery to make it pay. Enough prospecting had been done in the area to determine that the gold lay deeper than in Canada's Klondike and there were no easy pickings as there had been at Nome in 1900 when thousands made fortunes on the beaches. The realization that mining ground in Fairbanks was not "poor man's diggings," caused many stampeders to leave the region as quickly as they had arrived.

As a result, Fairbanks did not experience the explosive growth that marked earlier rushes to Dawson and Nome. By fall 1903, three sawmills were at work to satisfy the lumber demand and prospectors were combing the hills for gold. With key discoveries on Cleary, Ester and Fairbanks creeks, the town developed into a major gold mining center during the next 18 months. The city was incorporated in November 1903 and the newly elected city council chose one of its members, E.T. Barnette, as the first mayor.

▼ *The Metropolis of the Tanana still looks to its rivers as a source of prosperity. The pioneer Binkley family operates the riverboat* Discovery III *from their landing on Discovery Drive near the airport. The riverboat travels downstream on the Chena to the Tanana, then a short way down the Tanana to a camp where the lifestyle of the Athabaskan Indian is on display. The boat returns to its landing past some of the town's more exclusive homes that line the shores of the Chena. (Harry M. Walker)*

▼ *This building built in 1909 on the corner of First and Cowles once housed the George C. Thomas Memorial Library. Thomas, a Philadelphia banker and ardent Episcopalian who never visited Fairbanks, contributed $7,000 to construction and operation of the library. In 1925 the City of Fairbanks purchased the library for $1. The library remained here until the borough opened the new Noel Wien Public Library in 1981. The log building originally built to give miners at the Fairbanks Episcopal Mission a place to read and smoke is now on the National Register of Historical Places. (Steve McCutcheon)*

A young Scotsman, George Preston, arrived in Fairbanks on Jan. 4, 1904, about six weeks after leaving Valdez. "I thought for a while that we had, so to speak, 'jumped from the frying plan into the fire," because Fairbanks at that date was not much of a town."

There were a few saloons, the Northern Commercial Co. store and a smaller store, all lit by kerosene lamps and candles. After a hard winter on Fairbanks Creek, Preston returned to Fairbanks and got a job at the N.C. Co. as an assistant bookkeeper. He retired, as store manager, in 1947 at age 70.

When Preston went to work for the N.C. Co., the miners never paid in cash because there wasn't any, but there was enough gold dust by the spring to convince everyone that the strike was for real. "The dust was put up in Native-tanned caribou hide pokes, each holding 600 ounces. The company safe could not begin to hold our gold and we were given the use of an iron chest in the vault of the Fairbanks Banking Co.," he said.

By 1910, nearly $30 million in gold was produced from Cleary, Ester and Fairbanks creeks alone, almost two-thirds of the gold mined in the region. The richest gravels were buried beneath a thick layer of muck and tundra, and it took boilers and thawing equipment to develop the mines. Most of the work was done by drift mining in which shafts were sunk 20 to 80 feet down to reach the paystreak.

The trails to the creeks were notoriously bad, but transportation from Fairbanks took a giant step forward with the building of the Tanana Valley Railroad. The new railroad made it practical to bring in heavy boilers and other equipment to Fox, Cleary, Chatanika, Olnes, Gilmore and Vault. The trains originally ran from Chena, the town that competed with Fairbanks as a supply center.

Chena, at the mouth of the Chena River, had several advantages because it was easier to reach by riverboat, but it did not have the courthouse, which Wickersham had placed in Fairbanks. While Fairbanks grew, Chena faded away. By the end of World War I, rail commuter service to Chena stopped, and it wasn't long before the tracks were pulled up.

The railroad had been promoted by Falcon Joslin, a lawyer who envisioned the narrow-gauge rail line as the first link in a system that would eventually run east to Canada and west to the Seward Peninsula. Joslin predicted a great future for Fairbanks, but there were roadblocks on the path to progress.

Chief among them were the dual threats of flooding and fires. Starting in 1905, the Chena River flooded every five or 10 years and washed away homes and businesses. It wasn't until the flood control projects of the 1940s and the 1970s that the flood threat was eased. Fires were more irregular. While many bad ones occurred in winter when wood stoves were in use, the worst happened in spring. On May 22, 1906, a fire nearly obliterated the business section of what people in Fairbanks liked to call the "world's largest log cabin town."

The blaze began when a lace curtain swaying in the breeze in the window of a second-floor dentist's office came in contact with an alcohol lamp used to heat the dentist's instruments. The walls and ceiling caught fire and within minutes a huge plume of smoke arose from the three-story building on Cushman Street.

▲ *Today quiet streets in downtown Fairbanks display remnants of a by-gone era, when the hustle for gold turned a lonely trading post into a metropolis. (Harry M. Walker)*

"In those days Fairbanks did not boast of a paid fire department which could get the apparatus to the fire in a matter of seconds and there were no trained firemen," editor W.F. Thompson wrote later. "Everybody turned out and did the best they could, but it was an impossibility to quench the flames."

◀ *Samson Hardware is one of the oldest stores in Fairbanks, where you can still order a nut or bolt and the store clerks will run to the back and find the right size. Samson's joined the roster of pioneer businesses when James Barrack took control of a machine shop in 1912 that evolved into the hardware store. (Colleen Herning-Wickens)*

▶ *The Cushman Street Bridge crosses the Chena River near the original site of E.T. Barnette's trading post. Barnette's inability to travel by riverboat farther upstream on the Tanana River to a proposed trading site at Tanacross and discovery of gold in the hills north of Fairbanks led to the founding of Alaska's second largest city on a bend of the Chena River. (Harry M. Walker)*

The fire spread quickly to other buildings and roared through the business section of Fairbanks that afternoon and evening, causing damage estimated at $1.5 million. The businesses between First and Third avenues were wiped out. Attorney John Clark said that even before the ashes had cooled, people were ordering lumber and making plans to rebuild.

"As a fair example of the spirit with which the people met their losses, I well recall that of an old jeweler who lost everything but his violin. The other merchants and businessmen were comparatively young men and could start again, but he was well past middle age and it would be supposed that the future would look pretty black to him. My brother and I had an extra bed in the cabin where we were living, so we asked him to spend the night with us. He brought his violin and spent the early hours of the morning playing to us. He was as hopeful and buoyant of spirits as the youngest of them; rebuilt his store on borrowed money; afterwards went to Tanana, where he accumulated quite a substantial fortune before his death."

The headlines in the *Fairbanks News* the next day said: "Fire Can Not Stop Fairbanks" and "New and Better Town Arising from Smoking Ruins." The day after the fire the telegraph office took in nearly $700 as every merchant in town ordered new supplies from the states to replace what was destroyed.

By 1908, 3,500 people lived in the city and 15,000 more were spread out at small mining camps nearby, many of them connected by the Tanana Valley Railroad. Fairbanks had wooden sidewalks and muddy streets and it had become a modern town in the heart of Alaska.

Not mentioned in magazine articles or tourist brochures was the fenced "line," where the town's prostitutes lived in about 20 small cabins packed close together. The ladies of the line were allowed to continue in business as long as they paid fines to the city and did not solicit business in restaurants and saloons.

While everyone did not agree with what went on behind the high fence at Cushman Street and Fourth Avenue, the "line" was as

▲ *In some ways, having the federal courthouse in Fairbanks ensured the town's success. When Judge James Wickersham moved the seat of his Third Judicial District from Eagle to Fairbanks, E.T. Barnette donated the land for the new courthouse. The wooden original courthouse was replaced by this Art Deco monument in 1934. (Eric Rock)*

much a part of life in frontier Fairbanks as the town's other institutions.

There were three daily newspapers, a bookstore, a public school, two hospitals, a theater, curling club, five churches, a Masonic Lodge and various social clubs. Electric lights lit up the town and a telephone system connected 314 subscribers in Fairbanks and the surrounding mining camps. A long-distance call to Cleary Creek or Dome Creek cost $2.50 for five minutes in 1908.

The *Alaska-Yukon Magazine* said the Tanana Valley has many of the same characteristics as the Sacramento Valley, "but the Alaskan valley is larger and has a more fertile soil."

"The climate is not so severe as people imagine, and with direct railroad communication from seaboard to the valley the many resources of this part of Alaska would be rapidly developed and the valley would soon become the home of thousands of prosperous families," the magazine said.

Notwithstanding the fertile soil and climate, Fairbanks declined when gold production dropped off starting in 1910. The people in Fairbanks who longed for the good times to continue figured that the key might be better transportation, a railroad to the coast. When Congress approved construction of the Alaska Railroad in 1914, it was like a dream come true for the people in the Interior. They saw it as their hope for economic salvation.

In 1916, the Fairbanks Commercial Club published a pamphlet aimed at those outside the territory whose interest in Fairbanks had been sparked by excitement over the railroad.

"The railroad will bring about a condition to a certain extent paradoxical, for while Fairbanks will be made a greater mining camp it will at the same time be removed from the category of 'camps' in the usually accepted sense of the word and assume its rank as a 'town' of stability and assured permanence," the club said.

In 1916, Fairbanks had nine hotels, 20 lawyers, eight cigar stores, one architect, three dentists, two ice dealers, three civil engineers, seven doctors, 12 saloons and six billiard parlors. For recreation there was baseball in the summer, the highlight of which was the annual game played at midnight in the perpetual daylight of the longest day of the year. Forty members of the Fairbanks Lawn Tennis Club played at a wooden tennis court downtown while others enjoyed boat races, trap shooting, basketball, curling, skiing and snowshoeing. Sled dog races held great potential, everyone agreed.

"Last year a series of races was run here but Fairbanks has not yet taken the place it should as a dog-racing center," the club said. "This is something, however, that lovers of the sport hope to see corrected with time."

The 25-cent piece was the smallest coin in use and prices and wages were about double those in the states. "Nowhere in the world, perhaps, is the average workingman better fed and clothed and sheltered," Philip Knowlton wrote in *Sunset Magazine* in 1916. "The first to suffer from the decreased placer output of the district are the small merchants; for the number of business houses in operation in the old days is still maintained with little reduction, and the population is insufficient at present to warrant the continued existence of all of them."

A husband and wife could live comfortably on about $100 a month in 1916, but because of the decline in gold production, it was becoming more difficult to count on a steady income. More and more of the small cabins built during the gold rush were vacant. Business leaders quickly pointed out that there was still gold to be mined in the area, but the economic constraints were stifling mining.

Wood had always been the only fuel available for generating power and heat in Fairbanks. It was now getting so scarce on the denuded hillsides outside of Fairbanks that the price per cord had doubled and tripled.

The businessmen hoped new mining districts and the completion of the railroad would restore prosperity. Knowlton wrote that with modern transportation and access to cheap coal by rail from Healy, Fairbanks would thrive again as "the commercial and governing center of an immense district that will produce great wealth for coming generations."

A year after the railroad bill cleared Congress, Wickersham, as the territory's non-voting delegate, pushed a second piece of legislation through that would have an equally big impact on Fairbanks' future. In 1915, Congress approved legislation to create a land grant college in Alaska. It was the last bill to pass the 63rd Congress. With his own money, Wickersham paid for a cornerstone for the college and gave a 5,000-word speech at the dedication ceremony on July 4, 1915. Then Wickersham lobbied the Territorial Legislature to create a college to accept the land grant, which it did by one vote in 1917.

Fairbanks continued to shrink despite the promise that the railroad would open a new era for the college town. With the shutdown of so many small mines, people were leaving town because there was no other industry.

"There were empty cabins all over town, inhabited only by mud swallows nesting under the eaves," pioneer Clara Rust wrote.

"In those days Fairbanks was resting on past laurels without any new direction or impetus for progress. There was talk that Fairbanks would be like so many other boom towns — Dawson for example — that had its heyday and then died."

▼ *Second Avenue is decked out for Fourth of July in 1938. (Historical Photograph Collection, University of Alaska Fairbanks, courtesy of Dermot Cole)*

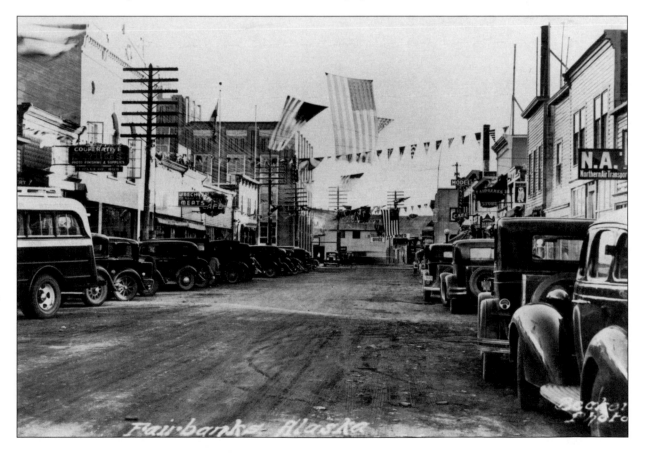

FAIRBANKS, ALASKA
NORTH END OF MAIN LINE
OF
THE ALASKA RAILROAD
THE NORTHERNMOST RAILROAD IN NORTH AMERICA

◀ Gold mining began to decline in Fairbanks about 1910 and the town's fathers blamed the decline partly on antiquated transportation in and out of Fairbanks. They saw the railroad as the savior of their prosperity. The Tanana Valley Railroad was built to connect Fairbanks with neighboring mines, but not until the federal government built the Alaska Railroad was Fairbanks connected by rail to any of Alaska's seaports. Now the modern line, owned by the state since the mid-1980s, links Fairbanks with Seward on the Gulf of Alaska. (Steven Seiller)

▶ Members of the Constitutional Convention held at the University of Alaska in the 1950s pose for this photo of the Fourth Division delegation. Back row from left are: John B. (Jack) Coghill, Ralph Rivers, Maurice Johnson, Robert McNealy, John Boswell and Les Nerland; front row, E.B. Collins, James Doogan, Ada Wien, Warren Taylor and George Cooper. (Steve McCutcheon)

During World War I, many men departed to join the Army or to seek work Outside. By 1920, the population had dropped to 1,100. Gold production in 1919 was down 92 percent from the peak in 1909. The war "bled Interior Alaska white in money and men, and a year ago Fairbanks reached its lowest ebb," the Tanana Publishing Co. said in a 1922 brochure about Fairbanks.

By then the long wait for the railroad ended. In July 1923, President Warren Harding visited Alaska and drove the golden spike at Nenana, signifying completion of the $65 million Alaska Railroad. Harding's visit was eagerly awaited and was the cause of much celebration. To mark the event, the name of Salchaket Lake, about 40 miles outside of town, was changed to Harding Lake. Harding rode through town, ate lunch at the Masonic Temple on First Avenue and visited the *Daily News-Miner*, where he set a line of type with his initials.

"When the President of the United States goes into a country newspaper office and sets type, thereby getting his fingers covered with dirt that almost won't come off, he is doing about all one fellow can do to distinguish one country print shop," editor W.F. Thompson wrote.

Harding said that no individual would have built the railroad, so it had to be done by the government. "I am glad a generous government understood and carried to completion the construction of the Alaska Railroad," he said at the Nenana ceremony. "It is not possible to liken a railway to a magician's wand, but the effect to me is the same. For the whole problem of civilization, the development of resources and the awakening of communities lies in transportation."

The rail connection to the coast meant that Fairbanks was able to get goods shipped north in a reliable fashion anytime during the year for about half the cost of river freight in summer. The transportation improvement,

▼ *The front page of the* Fairbanks Daily News-Miner *for Jan. 27, 1930, recounts the discovery of the wreckage of Carl Ben Eielson's plane in what was then the Soviet Union. (Courtesy of Eielson Air Force Base)*

coupled with a change in gold mining strategy revived gold mining in Fairbanks after World War I.

In a 1952 editorial, the *Daily News-Miner* said that two men deserved much of the credit for actions that helped bring new life to the town. They were Norman Stines, who in the mind of many Fairbanksans was synonymous with the Fairbanks Exploration Co., and Austin E. "Cap" Lathrop, who brought coal to Fairbanks along with movie theaters, a radio station and other enterprises.

Stines, from Boston, was a mining consultant who provided the vision and the energy for the ambitious mining plan that brought large-scale dredge operations to the Interior. He and Lathrop generated basic industry and steady payrolls for Fairbanks, helping sustain the community during the years leading up to World War II.

In the 1920s, when mining was no longer a pick-and-shovel proposition, Stines obtained options on placer mining properties throughout the Fairbanks area. Then he convinced investors that the properties did not contain "waste gold," but were rich in untapped wealth. All that was needed was a way to handle large amounts of low-grade gravel at a low cost.

Enter the massive dredges that operated round-the-clock for more than 250 days a year and were the lifeblood of Fairbanks for years to come. The mining claims were drilled to determine their value. Then in the summer the overburden was washed away with water from powerful nozzles called "hydraulic giants."

To obtain the water needed to wash away 10 feet to 100 feet of overburden, the mining promoters built the Davidson Ditch to bring water to Cleary, Goldstream and other creeks from the headwaters of the Chatanika River. The power to run the Fairbanks Exploration Co. dredges came from coal that could now be delivered via the Alaska Railroad. The coal deliveries were sporadic until Lathrop bought a controlling interest in the mine.

Lathrop, who moved to Fairbanks in the 1920s, had spent more than two decades building substantial enterprises in Cordova and Anchorage. In the years up to World War II and beyond, until his death in 1950, Lathrop did more than anyone else to change the face of Fairbanks. He built the first concrete building, the Empress Theater, which was completed in 1927 and withstood the climate and objections from skeptics who said the concrete would crack in the cold. He later built the Lathrop Building across the street on Second Avenue and the Lacey Street Theater. He also owned the newspaper, the *Daily News-Miner*, and the first radio station, KFAR.

By bringing a secure fuel supply to Fairbanks, Lathrop boosted the revival of gold mining. Now the dredges could run and there was an easy way of transporting dredge parts, draglines and later, bulldozers.

One of the keys to the new prosperity came in 1934 when President Franklin Roosevelt devalued the dollar and raised the price of gold to $35 an ounce. This made mining more profitable and created jobs. In 1935, when Fairbanks had a population of about 2,780, the Fairbanks Exploration Co. had 903 employees and a payroll of $1.9 million. A 1937 employment census listed 779 unemployed persons in the territory. In the Fairbanks district, two people were listed as totally unemployed and three as partially unemployed.

By the late 1930s, the town had taken on a more permanent look, with the addition of concrete government office buildings, the removal of the wooden sidewalks on Cushman Street and the $58,390 contract to make a five-block stretch of Cushman the first paved street in northern Alaska.

Despite the railroad, surface transportation remained a problem, and although Donald McDonald of Fairbanks urged construction of an international highway to connect Alaska with the United States, it took World War II to get the road built. Progress moved more quickly in air transportation because the Interior was an ideal place for flying.

Carl Ben Eielson, an Army Air Corps reservist, taught science in the Fairbanks high school and operated the first air mail flights in the territory in 1924. By the late 1930s, there were nearly four dozen airplanes flying out of Weeks Field and aviation had long since ceased to be a novelty. "In a way," Fairbanks mayor Les Nerland told a reporter in 1940, "Fairbanks is the most important aviation center in the world. Fairbanks people fly more miles per capita than any other people on earth. We are the hub of Alaska flying and we constitute one of the most important aviation crossroads of the Northern Hemisphere. The skies are our

most practical highways."

In addition to local fliers, the Fairbanks airfield was a stopping point for Wiley Post, Howard Hughes and others on round-the-world flights. The technological advances that had allowed civilian aviation to thrive brought another change to Alaska, one that was not immediately noticed. Because of the airplane, the isolation that had kept Alaska a world apart for so long had vanished.

During World War I, Fairbanks was a backwater on the verge of economic collapse. During World War II, Fairbanks was on the front lines of American defenses, a change

▲ *Steve and Jana Torrance canoe the Chatanika River, source of water for mining operations in the many creeks north of Fairbanks in the early days. Miners built the Davidson Ditch to route water from the Chatanika's headwaters to Cleary, Goldstream and other creeks where hydraulic nozzles washed away the muck overlying the gold. (Craig Brandt)*

that did more than anything since the original gold strike to create a new boom in the Metropolis of the Tanana. ■|

Les Nerland: The Sweet Life in Fairbanks

By Tricia Brown

Editor's note: *A former resident of Fairbanks, Tricia is the managing editor of* Alaska Magazine.

A good citizen. Call it an old-fashioned term, but it's still the best way to describe late Fairbanks businessman Arthur Leslie "Les" Nerland. He was viewed as an honest merchant, a fair employer, a hard-working family man. For many people, that kind of a reputation would be enough to rest upon. But Nerland didn't see it that way. He operated under the principle that giving to the community held much more benefit than could be measured in the books at the end of the best day at Nerland's Home Furnishings.

During his 62 years in

This portrait, taken in 1976 on the occasion of his 50th wedding anniversary, shows Les Nerland as patriarch of a business enterprise that would stretch from Alaska to Hawaii and Washington state. (Courtesy of the Nerland family)

Fairbanks, he poured himself into civic organizations and city government. He helped write the state's Constitution, and he sat on the governing board of the University of Alaska. Through a half-century of volunteer service, he helped shape the future of Alaska.

Out of the public eye, Les Nerland helped people, quietly assisting those who needed a hand, ensuring that the pioneers, the early Alaskans like his own father, were cared for. When Nerland died in 1992, a month short of his 90th birthday, Gov. Walter Hickel ordered state flags to half-mast and hailed Nerland for his contribution to the state. He was remembered as a man who loved his family, his city and his state, and therein was his legacy.

Les Nerland was born in Dawson City, Yukon Territory, on March 11, 1902, the only child of Andrew and Annie Nerland. The couple were Scandinavian immigrants who first met in Seattle, even though they had been raised in neighboring valleys back in Norway. Andrew Nerland was an entrepreneur, ever-ready for adventure and gifted with good business sense. He had crossed the ocean by cattle boat and steamer, enduring coarse accommodations and nearly inedible food, in the hope of a sweet life in the United States. He found what he sought.

Andrew and his partners, the Anderson brothers, were among the gold seekers who climbed Chilkoot Pass in 1898, five days after an avalanche buried 100 people. Upon arrival at Lake Bennett, the trio built a boat and sailed for the Klondike. There they decided it was too late to stake a claim, but they had another plan: Money could be made in the trade they already knew, painting and wallpapering. Homes were springing up everywhere in the boom town of Dawson, and homemakers didn't want to look at rough log interior walls. All told, in six months Nerland made three trips over formidable Chilkoot Pass, bearing paint, wallpaper and supplies. When he was settled, Annie joined him.

By 1904, the Fairbanks gold rush was in earnest, and the three men were ready to follow the other boomers. Fearing there would be no proper

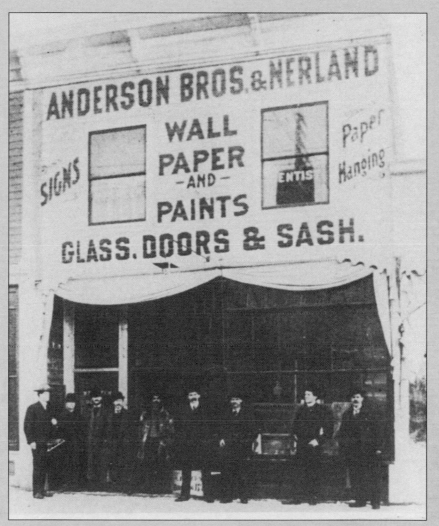

community for a wife and child, Andrew sent Annie and young Les back to Seattle. During the next few years, the business flourished in Fairbanks and, for brief periods, more stores were opened in Iditarod and Nenana.

Andrew bought out the Andersons, and took over the operation in 1922.

As Les was growing up, he saw his father each winter when Andrew came south for several months at a time. Back in

Fairbanks, Andrew was a leader in the Masonic Lodge, the Elks, Odd Fellows, Pioneers of Alaska and the Presbyterian church. He was instrumental in establishing and overseeing the Alaska Agricultural College and School of Mines, predecessor to the University of Alaska Fairbanks. He was city mayor, served on the city council and was elected to the Territorial Legislature seven times, where his last term of office ended when he was 80.

Les spent his youth in Seattle and earned a business degree from the University of Washington. In 1926, the tall young man married Mildred Kildall, and they began a family. Also that year Annie finally left Washington to join Andrew in Fairbanks. She proved an ideal business partner. Nerland's, on Cushman Street across from the post office, continued to thrive.

Like many other longtime Fairbanksans, Les and Mildred Nerland came north for what was supposed to be a short trip, and ended up staying for a lifetime. They had been invited to come for a year, to fill in for Andrew and Annie at the store. By the time his parents returned from their visit to Norway in 1930, their son was ready to call Fairbanks home and assume partnership in Nerland's.

He also assumed a major role in the community. As mayor between 1938 and 1940, Les Nerland saw that Fairbanks got its first paved streets and modern sewer system. He dined with Wiley Post the night before his fatal plane crash. He greeted Howard Hughes, who had stopped in Fairbanks during his around-the-world flight. All the while, he worked long hours at the store.

In passing the baton to his son, little did Andrew know that the move would launch a new era in the family business. Within 40 years, the small operation would catapult into a multimillion dollar corporation with stores thousands of miles apart in three states, each of them operated by grandchildren of Andrew Nerland.

World War II brought an influx of military personnel to Fairbanks, and Nerland's was there to meet their home furnishing needs. Les also led the Alaska Territory in sales of war bonds as part of the war effort.

Only child of pioneers Andrew and Annie Nerland, Les Nerland was born in Dawson City, Yukon Territory. When his father opened a branch of the family's home furnishings business in Fairbanks in 1904, young Les went to Seattle with his mother because his father thought the fledgling settlement might not be a suitable place for his wife and son. Mother and child settled in the Capital Hill area where Nerland put in his time as one of the "boys of summer." (Courtesy of the Nerland family)

After the war, under Les's guidance Nerland's expanded to a 15,000-square-foot, three-story building between Third and Fourth avenues in Fairbanks. The move was completed in 1953, after 49 years in the original location. The new building included a top-floor apartment for Les and his family, plus accommodations for Andrew and Annie on the second floor.

Many Fairbanksans fondly remember the shortcut from Second Avenue to Third, through the Co-op Drug Store, then Third to Fourth Avenue, through Nerland's, as a welcome respite from the bitter cold. Les didn't mind all the foot traffic, says his eldest son, Jerry. It just gave them all the more opportunity to make a few sales as the people passed through.

In 1955, Les was elected a delegate to the Alaska Constitutional Convention. Andrew was especially pleased because in 1917, while serving in the Territorial Legislature, he had introduced a bill advocating statehood. On Feb. 6, 1956, the last day of the convention, Les brought his copy of the document home to show his

85-year-old father. He remembered his father saying: "This is a big step toward statehood." Fifteen minutes later, Andrew collapsed and died. Annie lived six more years before her death at age 92.

With the death of the family patriarch, the passing of the baton was even more final. Still, Les and Mildred never pressed their daughter and two sons to follow in the footsteps of the family business. Yet that's just what happened. And their successes accelerated in the next two decades with new stores in Anchorage, Maui and Seattle.

In retirement from daily business operations, Les continued to serve the community. For 18 years, he worked on the Pioneers Home Board, which oversees management of several homes for Alaska's senior citizens. In 1979, the Alaska State Chamber of Commerce named Les "Outstanding Alaskan of the Year." In 1980, he received an honorary doctorate in public service from the University of Alaska. Also, like his father, he was bestowed the highest

honorary rank of the Scottish Rite Masonry, 33rd Degree.

Following the trail blazed by their pioneering forefathers, the children and grandchildren of Les Nerland continue to carry the torch of business and community service in Alaska. While the original stores are no longer in operation, the name remains in the public eye through new businesses created by the fourth generation.

The Nerland offspring remember their father and

grandfather as Bapa, the gentle, loving elder who, although he gave of himself in every direction, still belonged solely to them.

At his passing, an editorial in the *All-Alaska Weekly* noted: "Mr. Nerland had many friends throughout Alaska who will miss him, and who will remember him in gratitude for all he did."

Family, friends and many happy years. Like his father, Les Nerland had found a sweet life in Fairbanks.

Community service has long been a motto of the Nerland family. Here Andrew Nerland, front row center, poses with other delegates to the 10th Territorial Legislature in 1931 in Juneau. Andrew Nerland originally entered the home furnishings business in 1898 with Louis and Herman Anderson and their Anderson Bros. store in Dawson City, which later became Anderson Bros. and Nerland. In 1906 the Dawson store closed, but the Fairbanks store thrived, and in 1920 the company opened a branch in Nenana. In 1922 Andrew Nerland bought out the Andersons and the following year the Nenana branch was sold to the Northern Commercial Co. (Steve McCutcheon)

FAIRBANKS NORTH STAR BOROUGH

ALASKALAND

PIONEER PARK

CIVIC CENTER

PLAYGROUND

PICNIC AREA

The Golden-Heart City

By L.J. Campbell

World War II Comes to the Tanana

If gold mining birthed Fairbanks, then the military kept it going.

Fairbanks' first military base, Ladd Army Air Base, opened in 1940 as a cold-weather testing station for airplanes. The $4 million construction project started a tradition of government spending on which Fairbanks depends.

◀| *One of the biggest attractions for visitors and residents is Alaskaland, on a bend in the Chena River. Several museums, the restored sternwheeler* Nenana, *the rail car in which President Warren G. Harding rode to Nenana to officially conclude construction of the Alaska Railroad, and the Crooked Creek & Whiskey Island Railroad highlight the 44-acre pioneer theme park. (Roy M. Corral)*

Today, almost every other working person in the Fairbanks North Star Borough works for the government. In 1993, this included about 7,850 uniformed military personnel, 2,350 civilians employed on the military bases, another 890 people working for other federal agencies, about 4,250 people working for state government (primarily the University of Alaska) and some 2,700 local government employees. Even without including the uniformed military, government still accounts for 35 percent of the jobs here.

So how did the Army and Air Force come to be such a force in Fairbanks?

Throughout the 1930s, military strategists and territorial officials argued that Alaska should be fortified as part of the nation's defense network, particularly with the development of long-distance aircraft, according to Air Force historian John Haile Cloe in *Top Cover for America* (1984). Besides that, the U.S. Army Air Corps desperately needed pilots and planes capable of flying in arctic conditions.

One of the most experienced arctic pilots had been Carl Ben Eielson, a former Army pilot who settled in Fairbanks to teach high school. He flew the first air mail delivery into Alaska's Interior and then gained national recognition in 1928 when he flew across the arctic basin, from Point Barrow to the Spitsbergen Archipelago of Norway. Returning to Fairbanks, he started the commercial Alaskan Airways. But in 1929, Eielson crashed and died on the Chukotsk Peninsula coast of Russia's Far East, while attempting to recover passengers and cargo from a stranded schooner.

In 1934, the Army Air Corps took over mail flights in Alaska, and quickly racked up a dismal record. Dozens of crashes and fatalities plagued the corps that winter. A cold

▲ *Maj. Wyatt Fleming prepares his OA-10 Thunderbolt II aircraft for takeoff on a training mission from Eielson Air Force Base. He is receiving last minute checks from the ground crew and fellow pilots before closing the canopy and taxiing to the runway. Maj. Fleming is wearing the standard equipment for a military pilot, including fire resistant flight suit and gloves, plus survival vest, parachute harness, oxygen mask and flight helmet with visor. (Charles Newman)*

weather training and testing facility was needed more than ever, insisted military officials as they repeatedly pressed Congress for money to build Alaska airbases. Meanwhile, the world situation deteriorated. Construction on Ladd Field finally started in summer 1939, only months before the outbreak of World War II in Europe. Fairbanks, with its dependably frigid winters and a town to support construction, was a logical site.

Fliers at Ladd stayed busy at first diagnosing the particulars of northern aviation. They tried to adapt skis, like those used on bush planes, to their heavier bombers and fighters. They learned to deal with the effects of cold on airplanes and their bodies, even when flying through subzero temperatures in fabric-covered or open cockpits. Cloe writes that the first pilots to arrive at Ladd in September were bundled in fur-lined boots and jackets and surprised to find Fairbanks residents dressed in regular clothing.

As the war intensified, Congress authorized construction of numerous airfields in Alaska, along with the Alaska-Canada Highway to provide an overland supply route to Fairbanks and other Alaska military outposts. The road construction and the expansion of Ladd Field gave many local residents better paying jobs than they could imagine. The town entered a new phase.

Surprisingly, Ladd's military radio operators weren't the first in Alaska to hear about the Japanese bombing of Pearl Harbor, which drew the United States into World War II in December 1941. Fairbanks broadcaster Augie Hiebert heard about it first, while scanning short-wave frequencies before starting his morning shift on KFAR radio.

Hiebert's news coup was another feather for the relatively new and jaunty KFAR radio station, an enterprise of wealthy industrialist Cap Lathrop. In 1939, the 1,000-watt KFAR came on the air, pene-trating the Interior with its locally produced entertainment shows, sports and news. One of its innovations was a radio bulletin board called "Tundra Topics," which aired an assortment of news and personal messages to people in remote locations, items such as airplane arrival times and who was coming to visit. Today, bush message programs are standard fare on Alaska radio stations.

In 1942, Ladd Field became the northern transfer station for the Lend-Lease program to Russia, an American ally at the time. It was part of the Alaska-Siberia Air Ferry Route, one of four routes established to supply Russia with arms against Germany. Russian pilots congregated at Ladd, awaiting new war machines that they flew home. Nearly 8,000 Lend-Lease airplanes came through Fairbanks before the program ended in 1945.

During this time, Russian pilots, engineers and some civilians took over about half the base including sleeping quarters, offices, hangars and shops. American interpreters spent hours translating for the Russians, sometimes cramming into cockpits with the pilots.

The Russians considered Ladd Field a "rest camp," because of its comforts relative to Siberian outposts, wrote American staff officer Otis E. Hays Jr. in his 1982 account of the period for *The Alaska Journal*. In

Fairbanks, the Russians found shopping heaven. At the modern Piggly-Wiggly supermarket and landmark stores like Samson Hardware, they snapped up all sorts of American goods — candy, soap, cosmetics, perfume, lingerie, shoes, even canned foods — which they wedged into outbound Russian aircraft.

Today, the facility that served as Ladd Army Air Base is known as Fort Wainwright, the nation's farthest north Army post. About 4,500 soldiers and 6,300 family members are assigned to the post. Another 2,700 Air Force personnel and about 4,200 family members are assigned to Eielson Air Force Base, 23 miles south of town, at the site of what was used as a storage yard during the war.

The military presence has been strongly felt, particularly through the 1960s as well as recently. For instance, the payroll for Eielson's military employees was about $127 million in 1994, with another $54 million awarded to local construction contractors.

In 1987, a buildup at Fort Wainwright's 6th Infantry Division (Light) brought about 400 soldiers plus their families to Fairbanks. Then in 1990, another 600 people, mostly senior officers, moved onto base with the completion of the division headquarters relocation to Fort Wainwright from Fort Richardson in Anchorage. These moves stimulated the area's economy, particularly the 1987 influx which helped cushion Fairbanks from an otherwise severe recession sweeping the state. Construction jobs both on and off base boomed, and several big retailers moved to town. Vacant rental prop-erties suddenly had new tenants, and more civilian jobs opened up on post.

Living with the military can have a down side, however.

For instance, the late-1980s buildup at Fort Wainwright came at a time when local government, strapped for money, started slashing services. Schools became more

▼ *U.S. Air Force Tech. Sgt. Jose M. Duch inspects an OA-10 "Warthog" attack jet after a training mission. He is reviewing the pilot's "write-ups" regarding the way the aircraft performed during flight, and any discrepancies that may need maintenance attention. The maintenance hangar bays are visible in the background. (Charles Newman)*

crowded with the added military students. The city's small police force worried about more crime, with a new bunch of young soldiers added to the mix. Some residents didn't like the idea of sharing the area's fish and game with more military hunters. Even politicians fretted about how the big blocks of military voters might influence local elections.

Its dependency on the military makes Fairbanks particularly vulnerable to federal budget cuts. Alaska's small but powerful congressional delegation effectively shielded

Eielson and Fort Wainwright from massive drawdowns during the early 1990s, when the Clinton administration was shrinking the military and closing bases to cut costs. Even so, Fort Wainwright didn't completely escape. In 1994, the 6th Infantry was downgraded from a division to a brigade as part of the federal defense cutbacks, and some 600 soldiers and families moved out.

Today, the 6th Infantry remains the major unit at Fort Wainwright, with a number of battalions and companies from other Army infantries assigned here, too. Also located at

Fort Wainwright are the Bassett Army Community Hospital and the U.S. Army Cold Regions Research and Engineering Laboratory. The hospital serves more than 10,000 people, including those from Eielson and Fort Greely, an Army base located east of Fairbanks at Delta. The cold regions laboratory is one of four research and development laboratories nationwide for the U.S. Army Corps of Engineers.

Each summer, Fort Wainwright troops train on Alaska glaciers, and each winter they participate in Northern Edge arctic survival exercises. Sometimes the troops trade in their insulated boots and parkas for warm-weather gear, as they did for Operation Desert Shield in Saudi Arabia in summer 1990 and again in 1992 when they helped in the Philippines following a devastating volcanic eruption.

South of town, Eielson Air Force Base has grown exponentially since its initial

◄ *The military plays an important role in Fairbanks' economy. This influence stems primarily from the U.S. Army's Fort Wainwright and the U.S. Air Force's Eielson base. This field artillery unit is from Fort Wainwright. (U.S. Army)*

▶ *F-16s wait on the flight line at Eielson Air Force Base. The U.S. Air Force and U.S. Navy use the F-16s (Fighting Falcons) as multirole fighters. The plane can perform in poor weather and can fly more than 500 miles, complete its mission and return to home base. (Charles Newman)*

▲ *Construction began on what was then Ladd Army Air Base in 1939. Today the post is known as Fort Wainwright, the northernmost post of the U.S. Army and home to about 4,500 soldiers and the 6th Infantry Brigade. (U.S. Army)*

construction with two asphalt runways in 1943. Today, this large northern installation controls about 62,000 acres and hosts the 354th Fighter Wing, part of the 11th Air Force headquartered at Elmendorf Air Force Base in Anchorage. Active duty squadrons at Eielson fly OA-10 Thunderbolts and F-16 Fighting Falcon fighter planes. In addition, arctic survival training is given to all military branches through Eielson's "Cool School." Another detachment at Eielson operates and maintains part of the U.S. Atomic Energy Detection System through seismic monitoring and air testing. Still another unit handles vast volumes of freight aboard cargo planes.

Units of the Alaska Air National Guard operate air-to-air refueling tankers and search-and-rescue helicopters, also from Eielson.

During World War II, Eielson was known as "26 Mile" because of its proximity to a U.S. Army telegraph station, which was located at mile 26 of the Richardson Trail that linked Fairbanks with Valdez. The base functioned during the war primarily as a storage area for Lend-Lease aircraft from Ladd Field. In 1946, the base started expanding and in 1948, the name was changed to honor pilot Carl Ben Eielson. When Ladd was turned over to the Army and became Fort Wainwright in 1961, Eielson assumed some of the missions and units from Ladd.

In 1992, a volcanic eruption in the Philippines prompted closure of Clark Air Force Base and brought one of the Air Force's premiere air combat training exercises home to Eielson. This 10-day combat exercise, called Cope Thunder, occurs six times a year to give pilots, tactical and support crews simulated combat experience. Each Cope Thunder brings more than 500 people and 60 aircraft to Eielson for about a three-week stretch, drawing from bases all over the United States and foreign countries. During the exercises as many as 70 fighter jets may be flying in Alaska's airspace simultaneously.

Both Eielson and Fort Wainwright open some of their facilities to use by local civilians, such as the Army's golf course and Birch Hill ski area. In most respects, however, they are self-contained cities with on-site housing, libraries, grocery stores, shopping marts, laundries, salons, flower shops, fitness centers, theaters, medical clinics and schools. At the same time, the military helps in the civilian community, particularly in emergencies, and a number of Army and Air Force personnel take up permanent residence in Fairbanks or nearby communities like North Pole when they retire. ∎|

North Pole, Alaska - Where Dreams Come True

By Janice C. Noll

Editor's note: *Janice Noll teaches sixth grade at North Pole Middle School. The early history of North Pole was the topic for her master's degree project in Northern Studies at the University of Alaska Fairbanks.*

North Pole had its beginnings wrapped in the dreams of several families who came to Alaska as fortune hunters. The fortune they sought was not unlike that of most young couples who seek a future and name for themselves. Many of those who made a home in Alaska's North Pole traveled over the new highway that connected the territory with the Lower 48.

The Alaska-Canada (Alcan) Highway, a dirt and gravel road completed in 1942, was open to the public after World War II. Men who worked on the Alcan, as it was known then, returned to Alaska in search of their dreams. Many others traveled to Alaska in the late 1940s and early 1950s for adventure and new beginnings. Those who planned to stay found that the

available land around Fairbanks was swampy or already taken.

Homesteads were patented along the Richardson Highway, a road that connected Fairbanks with the Alcan. The land between 6 Mile and 26 Mile was in demand in the '40s and '50s because of its proximity to the two active military bases in the Tanana Valley.

One homestead couple was Bon Valjean Davis and his wife, Bernice. The Davises staked their homestead at 14 Mile on the Richardson Highway in

1944. After a rude log home was built, the Davis boys, Neil (12) and Lewie (8), arrived by plane to join their parents. The boys helped clear the homestead land, which proved to be quite a job given the stubbornness of the thick moss. When fall came, the boys were taught at home, since the drive to Fairbanks was not an easy one on the gravel, marshy, sometimes-one-lane Richardson Highway. The Davises received their patent in April 1949. Davis was a teacher before he arrived in Alaska but

North Pole's best-known landmark is Santa Claus House, a fantasyland filled with a potpourri of Christmas novelties. Children can send their letters to Santa here, where friendly elves do their best to make every visit memorable. (Charles Newman)

engaged in various other occupations to keep the homestead operational: road camp cook, baker, pig farmer, lumberman, land speculator and jail keeper.

James and Grace Ford were also significant homesteaders who received their patent in January 1951. Their land was on the south side of the Richardson Highway at 14 Mile. James Ford did not depend on the land to make a living. Although he considered himself a gentleman farmer and raised potatoes to sell to the military, Ford ran a refrigeration sales and repair business in Fairbanks. Grace Ford quit her post office position to remain on the homestead to raise their children.

The Davises and Fords are linked in history because on Jan. 16, 1953, the Davis homestead and 80 acres of the Ford homestead became the first city limits of the community known as North Pole, Alaska.

Newspaper articles of the early 1950s suggest that the plans to incorporate as a city were instigated and supported by Everett Dahl. Dahl was a realtor who, with his partner Kenneth Gaske, purchased all but 40 acres of the Davis homestead on Feb. 1, 1952. Once the deal was signed, the property was subdivided into small lots that were sold to military personnel from Fort Wainwright and Eielson Air Force Base, as well as others moving into the area.

Dahl was an acquaintance of Ethel Granite, a Fairbanks matron. Granite was determined to establish a Santa Claus home away from home, near Fairbanks, to draw tourists to Alaska's Interior. The name "North Pole" was linked to efforts of Granite and her friends Audree Vance and Vera Myatt. The three women sent a wooden, candy-striped pole to the geographic North Pole, Dec. 12, 1951, where it was dropped with a sack of letters to Santa from children all over the United States. The ladies, with support from organizations in New York and California, developed big plans to build a non-profit community in Alaska's Interior. The project would be known as Santa-Land and North Pole. They began the noble endeavor at various sites. One site was located six miles north of Fairbanks on the Steese Highway. Another was at 14 Mile on the Old Richardson Highway.

The North Pole name was tried on South Fairbanks in January 1952. Because South

Dan Coben Sr. of D & I Seed inspects sunflowers at his farm near North Pole. Coben operates a diversified crop farm that produces oats, barley, straw, grass seed and pea seed and does custom land clearing. The sunflowers are part of a University of Alaska Fairbanks research project on Coben's land that is investigating other potential economic crops. In this project the investigators are looking for early maturing varieties of sunflowers that might be suitable for the bird seed market. (Don Pitcher)

This aerial shows the layout of North Pole. The Tanana River is at lower right; the diagonal road running across the photo from lower left to upper right is the Old Richardson Highway. The current Richardson Highway is at extreme upper left. Fifth Avenue, the main cross street, extends from the Richardson Highway toward the lower right near the river. (Courtesy of Evolyn Melville)

Fairbanks was not included in the city limits, the residents wanted services that a city could provide. Some of the local folks held rallies to annex with Fairbanks; others wanted to incorporate as a separate city to be called North Pole. Both Ethel Granite and Everett Dahl favored South Fairbanks incorporating as "North Pole," but the petition for incorporation lacked the proper signatures so the scheme was dropped for South Fairbanks.

With Dahl's guidance, the area at 14 Mile started calling itself North Pole. In fact, one of the conditions of the purchase of the homestead from Bon Davis was that the name be changed from Davis to North Pole. Dahl encouraged Granite to build her Santa-Land project at 14 Mile. Due to lack of funds, Granite's plans

for Santa-Land faded and eventually were forgotten.

Unlike the South Fairbanks group, the residents at 14 Mile successfully petitioned to incorporate and held their first election on January 15, 1953. The vote was 20 for and three against incorporation. The first mayor of the City of North Pole was James Ford. Everett Dahl and Conrad (Con) Miller were chosen directors.

Con and Nellie Miller bought two lots from Dahl prior to incorporation in 1952 on which they built a gift and variety store. When the results

of the election were complete, the Millers named their store Santa Claus House. Santa Claus House has been the center of the city's tourist attractions ever since. The Millers and Fords have been influential in the community, contributing to its planning and growth. Both Con Miller and James Ford have served as mayors, trading places depending on the outcome of each election.

Today dreams are still made in North Pole. Children whisper their wish list to Santa while the grown-ups work hard to

improve their community. The city is the hub of a larger settlement that stretches along Badger Road to Moose Creek, a small community west of Eielson Air Force Base. There is definitely a "North Pole" of the mind, as many homeowners consider themselves living in North Pole although they reside outside the city limits.

The City of North Pole continues to grow. Beginning with 196 acres and approximately 90 residents, the modern city now covers just less than four square miles with a population of 1,671. Two oil refineries are located on the fringe of the city by the Tanana River. Three new malls have been built. The city has three schools and two parks. The 5th Avenue Park displays the actual pole that was retrieved from the geographic North Pole.

Part of North Pole's image was developed with the establishment of the Christian radio station known as KJNP, King Jesus North Pole. Established just outside the city limits by Don and Gen Nelson in 1967, the station has grown to include the broadcast of Christian television programs. North Pole has several churches within its city limits and many

|▶ Lew and Ruth Cunningham owned the North Pole Trading Post which stood at the corner of Fifth Avenue and Santa Claus Lane until it burned a few years ago. This photo was taken in the 1970s. (Courtesy of Evolyn Melville)

◀ In the mid-1970s Earth Resources built a petroleum refinery at North Pole. In 1981, Mapco Alaska Petroleum Inc. purchased the refinery, which processes 130,000 barrels of royalty oil from the state daily and produces 38,000 barrels of refined products such as gasoline for the Fairbanks and Anchorage markets, heating oil for the Interior, jet and aviation fuel for commercial and military use, and the export product naptha, a petrochemical feed stock that is a raw ingredient for petroleum-based products such as plastics. North Pole was selected as the site of the refinery because it was close to the trans-Alaska pipeline, and to the rail head at Fairbanks and because there was an obvious market in the Interior for heating oil and aviation fuel. (Mapco Alaska Petroleum)

more in the surrounding area.

The city has developed as a Christmas theme town with banners and decorations visible throughout the year. Tourists stop in North Pole to photograph the giant Santa located between the new SantaLand RV Park and the Santa Claus House Christmas store.

The community has grown in spite of its transient population. Families come for a while and then move away only to be replaced by other young families. The community's patriarchs are treasured because of their long dedication to improving and contributing to the betterment of the area. It is generally felt that North Pole is a terrific place to raise a family.

Several city events draw families together as does the availability of a community swimming pool located in the North Pole Middle School complex. Some of the events are the fall Candle-Light-Vigil, the Health Fair, the Winter Carnival and various activities at the elementary, middle and high schools, and the North Pole branch of the Noel Wien Public Library.

North Pole continues to be a place for dreams as is evident on the sign located at 5th Avenue and the New Richardson Highway:

Welcome to North Pole, Alaska
"The Home of Santa Claus"
...where dreams come true....

Higher Learning, Alaska-style

When the military arrived in Fairbanks, the University of Alaska was still a small, fledging school. The campus sat on College Hill, an ancient Athabaskan campsite on the outskirts of town, surrounded by woods and bordered by farms. Students and faculty drove dog sleds to class and tied their dogs in a field midcampus, until the president banned the practice because of the noisy yipping.

Aptly named the Alaska Agricultural College and School of Mines, the young school mirrored activities around it. Along with the miners, there were homestead farmers raising vegetables and grains for the community, increasingly populated by lawyers, doctors and merchants. Old pictures show hay wagons rolling through town, grain fields on Farmer's Loop Road, and greenhouses full

▼ *The university's Lower Campus overlooks these grain fields, crowded during fall migration with Canada geese and sandhill cranes. (Pat Costello)*

Early mining classes held in a practice mine under the campus were enhanced by field trips to operating mines. The experimental farm anchored the agricultural curriculum. Even after the college was renamed University of Alaska in 1935, to reflect the school's expanding activities, agriculture and mining education continued. A picture taken at the Agricultural Experiment Station in 1943 shows the 4-H Potato Club learning to sort spuds.

Today, crop courses are still taught and research specific to northern farming continues at experimental farms in Fairbanks and near Palmer, north of Anchorage. However, agriculture as a viable commercial industry in Alaska is essentially nonexistent, except for greenhouse operations and some truck farming. In the Fairbanks region, farmers grow potatoes, lettuce, cabbage and carrots, most sold locally. Some of them cultivate oats and barley as livestock feed, but efforts by the state to encourage large-scale grain farms in the Interior have failed.

In the meantime, the university's agricultural school has broadened its offerings to include outdoor recreation and park and wilderness management, appropriate considering the large percentage of public lands in Alaska.

The university's mining school followed the rise and fall of placer gold mining in the region. During the 1930s, the mining school boasted the largest enrollment of any department and was the "most professional and well-equipped department on the campus," writes historian Terrence Cole in *The Cornerstone on College Hill* (1994). But World War II drained the university of faculty and students, and the mining school closed for a year when gold production was declared a non-essential industry. The school adjusted to the changing times which soon brought geological and petroleum engineering to the forefront, reflecting Alaska's overwhelming dependence on oil. Mining still gets a portion of research dollars.

While the university started out as a land grant college, today it is a land-space-sea grant college, one of the few in the nation to be so designated. The sea grant came in 1970 from the National Oceanic and Atmospheric Administration. The university didn't get a parcel of ocean, but it got funding for oceanside research centers in Seward, Kodiak and Juneau. Then in 1991, the National Aeronautics and Space Administration bestowed space-grant status, recognizing work going on since 1948 at the university's Geophysical Institute and Poker Flat rocket range.

The Geophysical Institute is the core of the university's research and graduate programs, asserts historian Cole. One of the institute's big white buildings on campus wears a technological hat of satellite dishes, telescopes, meteorological instruments, cameras and antennas. Its scientists and graduate students study auroras, volcanoes,

of produce on Garden Island. The government established an experimental farm west of town in 1907 to determine what crops could be successfully grown here, in the nation's northernmost farming region.

Then came the college, authorized by Congress through the federal land grant program at the urging of Alaska's territorial delegate Judge Wickersham. The judge laid the cornerstone of the first building, even as the territorial legislature was acrimoniously arguing whether the mining camp of Fairbanks deserved a college. The school with one building finally opened seven years later, offering practical education in agriculture, mining and home economics to six students.

earthquakes, permafrost, glaciers, arctic haze, ice fog, ozone, global climate change, radiation and geothermal energy. At the institute's synthetic aperture radar facility, images from satellites are used to track and monitor all sorts of things, from oil spills and forest fires to glacier surges. Out at Poker Flat, about 30 miles north of campus, scientists launch unmanned rockets to collect information from space. At the range's optical observatory, sky watchers analyze northern lights and other atmospheric displays. The institute is also home to the world's largest super-computer, funded by a $25 million federal appropriation.

"There's a lot of very sophisticated stuff going on amidst these trees and mines," says Henry Cole, executive director of Interior Alaska Economic Development Council. He thinks Fairbanks has great potential to attract technical and aerospace firms because of the university's research base. As early as 1960, a master plan recommended that the university mold itself as the premiere arctic research institute, and this was a goal of President William R. Wood, who pushed for creation of numerous arctic research institutes at the university during his tenure.

Compared to a meager handful of students at its start, today about 7,000 students attend classes at the Fairbanks campus, with another 2,300 enrolled statewide. The university system, headquartered on the Fairbanks campus, includes the University of Alaska Fairbanks, two other separately accredited universities in Anchorage and Juneau, branch campuses, learning centers and extension offices in rural towns and villages throughout the state. UAF is the only unit offering doctoral degrees.

The university has always been plagued by the lack of funding. In the late 1940s, the university almost closed from bankruptcy, when the territorial budget skidded into the red. Tuition collected in advance

|▶ *The university's Large Animal Research Station, run by the Institute of Arctic Biology, conducts research on caribou, reindeer and musk ox. Most of the research focuses on nutrition and reproduction. This young moose (left) and caribou were part of the station's herd some years ago. In 1994 the station had no moose among its research animals. For a time, the station also raised caribou-reindeer hybrids, called "carideer" or "reinbou." The research was aimed at helping reindeer herders in western Alaska better manage their herds, which probably contained hybrids. Reindeer were introduced to Alaska about 100 years ago. They have shorter legs and don't migrate as extensively as caribou, and the two have different reproductive cycles. Yet they are similar enough to interbreed and produce fertile offspring. The last two hybrids at the station died in 1994. (Jay Schauer)*

and personal loans from Fairbanks business leaders kept the college open. In the late 1970s the university faced another financial crisis, and then another in the mid-1980s, when world oil prices plunged, cutting into state revenues generated from oil taxes.

Since then, the state legislature has continually whittled down its share of the university's funding. Practically all components of the university system have suffered, including full-time faculty and programs. Maintenance of the Fairbanks campus has been critically deferred, and now leaky roofs, antiquated electrical and mechanical systems, and safety code violations plague many older buildings. At the same time, more on-campus housing and classrooms are needed. University officials in 1993 toyed with the idea of raising money by leasing university farmland to commercial developers who wanted to build a grocery and shopping mart. The plan died in the face of public outrage.

Yet despite its budget woes, the university is nationally recognized for research, funded

◀| *The Rawson sisters, Megan (4) and Leslie (2) enjoy the flowers at the university's Georgeson Botanical Garden. (Roy M. Corral)*

|▶ *Dr. William R. Wood, president of the University of Alaska from 1960 to 1973, has been a leader in education and Fairbanks civic affairs for more than three decades. (Roy M. Corral)*

mostly by grants. It is one of the top 100 universities nationwide, of 3,700 applying each year, in funding received from the National Science Foundation and gets more money for arctic research than any of the others. Total research dollars from all sources in 1994 approached $48.4 million, or about 79 percent of all non-state money brought into the university system. More than 10 percent of the university's students come from the Lower 48, many drawn by its science and engineering programs.

The university's location on the edge of some of the world's most challenging wilderness may be another attraction for students. In 1988, *Outside* magazine declared UAF

the "ultimate adventure school."

Over at the university's Alaska Native Language Center, linguists and oral historians document Alaska's human side, recording and preserving languages, stories and traditions of Alaska's many indigenous people. Historian Cole notes that the center, which has published nearly 250 titles in 19 languages during the past two decades, may well be the University of Alaska's "most original contribution to the world of knowledge."

Along with academics and research, the university at Fairbanks has been a top contender in some sporting circles for several decades. The men's and women's rifle teams constituted an "intercollegiate target shooting

dynasty" in the 1960s, wrote Cole. Recent times have been little different: In 1994 its rifle team won the NCAA national rifle championship. The university's skiers compete nationally, as do its basketball teams and in 1994, its Nanooks hockey team was

▼ *The Butrovich Building houses the new supercomputer at the University of Alaska Fairbanks. The building was named for businessman, politician and Fairbanks pioneer John Butrovich, who was born at Fairbanks Creek in 1910. Butrovich served on the Fairbanks City Council and in the territorial Senate. (Don Pitcher)*

admitted to the Central Collegiate Hockey Association of the NCAA. This was a big deal for the town, as well as the university.

Hockey has been popular in Fairbanks since the town's early days. Women, men and children played then on the frozen Chena River, setting up makeshift rinks with bleachers for spectators. The hockey season lasted from freeze-up until breakup, when the river ice went out. Today, adult and youth skaters hone their skills at outdoor school rinks and the indoor Big Dipper, while the Nanooks and the Fairbanks Gold Kings, a senior men's team on the national amateur circuit, play at Carlson Center. This borough-owned sports complex, located on the banks of the Chena

River, hosts an array of athletic competitions and community events year-round.

One of the most popular places on campus is the university's museum, located on the southwest edge of College Hill. The museum is officially named after Otto Geist, an amateur paleontologist and archaeologist, who collected massive quantities of artifacts and fossils in Alaska and collaborated with the university's first president, Charles Bunnell, to create the museum.

Today, the museum is one of the first places many Fairbanks residents take their guests, and it regularly gets bus loads of tourists. The view from outside the museum overlooks the city and valley beyond, with the Alaska Range and Mount McKinley looming on the southern horizon on clear days. Exhibits practically spill out the museum's front door, luring visitors into the galleries. Permanent displays of mounted wildlife specimens, natural history, minerals, Native art and history, arctic science and contemporary art fill the main floor. The museum hosts traveling exhibits and special events as well, with information on upcoming events available at the museum gift shop.

The university also infuses the city with cultural events and a diversity of people that otherwise might well be absent in a town of Fairbanks' size and relative remoteness. Symphony performances, lectures, theater productions and the annual summer arts festival are some of the university's cultural contributions. As Ginny Wood, a long-time Fairbanks resident said about the university: "It keeps us from being jerkwater." ■|

The Permafrost Tunnel: Alaska's Prehistoric Root Cellar

By Sean Reid

Editor's note: Sean is a free-lance writer from Anchorage.

It may smell like a pair of old gym socks left in the refrigerator, but it feels more like a time tunnel, a 360-foot-long tunnel carved from the eternally frozen ground near Fairbanks that descends into a prehistoric time of saber-toothed cats. Here in the permafrost tunnel researchers find bones ± 15,000 years old and wood from 15,000 to 40,000 years old.

The tunnel was dug by the U.S. Army Corps of Engineers in the 1960s at a site adjacent to a large valley thoroughly dredged during placer mining early this century. The engineers used tunneling machines to bore into a hillside known to contain ice-rich permafrost. Like placer miners 50 years earlier, they encountered ancient bones and plant remains as they worked their way through centuries of accumulated silt and gravel in old river beds.

But it wasn't the lure of ancient bones that drew the

Corps to this site some 30 years ago. U.S. Army Cold Regions Research and Engineering Laboratory engineers constructed the tunnel in several stages to evaluate methods for underground excavation in frozen soil. They also studied tunnel behavior in permafrost: tunnel deformation, natural air flow and the thermal regime, which is the relationship of air and ground temperature in a tunnel. The main horizontal

A 360-foot tunnel dug into a hillside near Fairbanks provides clues to past environments. Bones of prehistoric mammals, some 15,000 years old, and wood fragments, some as old as 40,000 years, have been found embedded in the tunnel's walls. (Sean Reid)

tunnel was bored with giant, modified augerlike mining equipment. Later, engineers from the U.S. Bureau of Mines excavated a smaller adit to reach a layer of gravel slightly below the predominantly silty layer of the main tunnel. As engineers found out, hard-to-excavate frozen gravel needs to be thawed or blasted. However, it turns out that frozen silt is relatively easy to excavate or trench while it remains frozen. But if it thaws, "you're in deep trouble," reports

Dr. Nils Johansen, professor of geological engineering at University of Alaska Fairbanks.

Today, the Bureau of Mines and the Corps of Engineers maintain and operate the facility as an active underground laboratory.

Warm air is perhaps the tunnel's biggest threat. While Fairbanks winters are notorious for temperatures that can plunge to minus 40 degrees or below for weeks, summers can be surprisingly warm with weeks

in the 70s and 80s under near-continuous daylight. To preserve the permafrost, the tunnel is chilled in winter by natural convection with cold air entering through the entrance portal and exiting through a small ventilation shaft at the far end. In summer, a mechanical refrigeration system is used to keep the tunnel entrance cool. To guard against underground warming, even the long strings of incandescent light bulbs that illuminates the shaft are turned off

whenever they are not needed. The tunnel remains a fairly constant 26 degrees year round.

Driving to the tunnel site, invited guests are greeted by a small sign and a locked gate a few yards down a gravel road off the highway. A portable building left over from the Corps' construction days serves as a gathering spot where visitors are briefed, shown a simple cross-sectional diagram of the tunnel and asked to don hard hats. Hunching over to enter through a small door in what appears to be a nondescript backyard shed, a visitor is greeted with the cool, heavy air of some place old, dark and stale. It smells like — well, old gym socks in a refrigerator.

Beams reinforce the first few feet of the tunnel. The floor is a gently sloping layer of smooth ice made from water that entered the tunnel and froze. Covering the ice is an extremely fine layer of silty dust from the

Permafrost claims this recently demol-ished house along Farmer's Loop Road. One of the reasons for construction of the permafrost tunnel was to study conditions contractors would face in building over permafrost. (Roy M. Corral)

walls and ceiling that is kicked up with each step. Deeper into the tunnel, a visitor is surrounded by jagged, organic-rich walls. Reaching farther into the hillside and gradually descending through layers of silt, gravel and time, the artifacts of eons reveal themselves. The walls and ceiling are strewn with antediluvian tree roots, tundra peat, large ice wedges, a burned log, ancient bison bones, a cross section of a prehistoric pond, 40,000-year-old tree stumps, and even bones from a saber-toothed cat. These remains are not mineralized, just frozen.

Radiocarbon dating of fragments of bones, wood, and peat and fibrous plant materials tells the geologic and climatic history of the region.

The youngest layers exposed in the tunnel reveal a period about 11,000 years ago. Plant roots and tundra remains at about 36 feet beneath the surface date to about 30,000 years ago, to a time when Alaska's Interior was cold and dry. Here, too, are found most of the bison and caribou remains. In the gravel about 56 feet below the surface are found the stumps of an ancient forest washed to this location by a river about 40,000 years ago.

The variety of ice formations and types exposed in the walls are also of considerable interest because they reveal information about ice structures themselves and also about the environment that existed when they formed. The ice wedges, some much more than 3 feet wide, tell of growth cycles spanning thousands of years. Trapped bubbles in the ancient ice may lead to a better understanding of the Earth's atmosphere long before industrial pollution.

Engineers also study the ice-rich permafrost itself to understand problems associated with construction in and on frozen soils and in ice structures such as wedges. Much of what was learned in the permafrost tunnel was put to use in engineering the 800-mile trans-Alaska oil pipeline in the 1970s. Heeding the lesson that permafrost soil best be kept frozen, engineers insulated or elevated the 48-inch pipe where it traversed permafrost. Because the route of the pipeline takes it across hundreds of miles of discontinuous permafrost, about half of the pipeline sits on refrigerated vertical support members or piles several feet above the ground. Where buried but improperly insulated, the pipeline has in

places begun to sag as the heat from the oil within has caused melting of the surrounding non-thaw-stable permafrost.

The tunnel itself is undergoing some structural deformation. About 300 feet into the tunnel, the ceiling is slowly collapsing toward the floor. The rate of this permafrost creep is being studied by Dr. Johansen and his colleagues, who, by better understanding the dynamics of permafrost, can help engineers and architects design better structures and roads. Intrigued and somewhat bemused by builders who think simply adding more ground insulation will solve problems associated with construction in

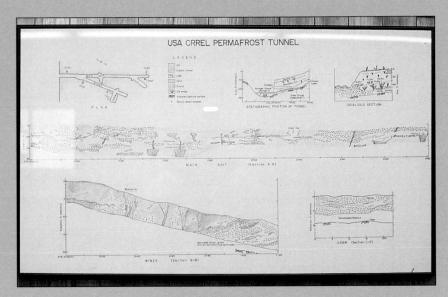

This schematic shows the layout of the permafrost tunnel. (Sean Reid)

ice-rich permafrost areas, Dr. Johansen cautions: "You cannot stop the transfer of heat, you can only slow it down. No matter how much insulation you use."

While the Fairbanks permafrost tunnel continues to be the subject of scholarly interest and general curiosity, it is not yet open to the casual visitor. For the time being, the frozen bones and chilled, pungent air of Alaska's version of the time tunnel remain the domain of a lucky few in the academic underground.

Mining the Myths

So with Fairbanks mostly a government town today, what happened to all the miners?

It has been decades since Fairbanks swarmed with prospectors. At the height of gold mining during the 1910s, more than 3,000 miners worked in the Fairbanks Mining District alone, an area roughly corresponding to the modern borough. Lots of miners also lived in the surrounding districts, such as Circle with its gold mine boomtown Circle City, and Richardson and Bonnifield districts, also in the borough.

Fairbanks' early growth shared mining's ups and downs. By the 1920s, less than 500 miners remained in Fairbanks, but the 1930s brought a gold mining surge. The big earth-moving dredges of Fairbanks Exploration (F.E.) Co. arrived about the time gold prices skyrocketed, and the industry revived temporarily. Some 1,600 people worked in mining. But by 1942, the military was firmly entrenched in Fairbanks, and mining took a back seat to government, although the dredges continued to produce gold through the 1950s.

Today, gold mining plays a relatively small part in the overall Fairbanks economy. The military, the university, other government agencies, groceries, department stores, medicine, even construction and oil employ more people in the Fairbanks region than does gold mining.

The two leading employers behind government are retailers and service providers. Some 6,000 people, about 20 percent of those employed in the borough, work in stores, groceries, restaurants and bars. Many of these jobs came in the early 1990s with a retail boom that brought several large national chains to town. Sears, Fred Meyer, Pace and Kmart all built large new stores. Another 7,000 people, or about 23 percent of the total, work in health, social and business services including hotels. These numbers partly reflect Fairbanks' importance as a hub for the Interior.

In comparison, mining accounted for less than 2.5 percent of total borough employment in 1994. Of the borough's 700 mining jobs, a monthly average, only about 120 were in gold mining.

The bulk of the borough's mining jobs were in petroleum oil and natural gas, a mining subcategory that includes drilling outfitters and oil company employees. Oil and gas are the leading revenue producers statewide, because of the North Slope oil fields.

◄| *Visitors listen to information on the trans-Alaska pipeline at the Alyeska Visitor Center near Fairbanks. The pipeline is made of high, tensile-strength carbon steel pipe 48 inches in diameter with walls 1/2-inch thick. (Pat Costello)*

Big changes came to Fairbanks, like many other places in the state, with the discovery of oil at Prudhoe Bay in 1968. Construction of the trans-Alaska pipeline, to carry the oil south to Valdez for shipment to out-of-state refineries, the largest private construction project ever proposed, seemed imminent with news of the oil strike. Numerous Fairbanks businesses borrowed money to buy inventory for the anticipated boom. But various environmental and legal challenges to the pipeline, including settling disputes about land claims with Alaska's Natives, delayed construction until 1974, and many Fairbanks businesses went bankrupt during the wait.

Fairbanks did eventually become a head-quarters for pipeline construction and when that happened, money and people flowed through town like nothing seen before or since. For better than four years, Fairbanks served as the hiring, management, transportation and supply center for the northern two-thirds of the pipeline. Alyeska Pipeline Service Co., the oil company consortium that owns the pipeline, pumped an estimated $200,000 to $500,000 a day into the local economy during construction, according to Mim Dixon in her comprehensive analysis of the period in *What Happened to Fairbanks* (1978).

The construction boom brought thousands of people to town looking for high-paying pipeline jobs: Laborers and skilled craftsmen made $1,000 to $1,500 a week. Crowds clogged the town and locals found themselves waiting in traffic, grocery lines and at the post office. People not only came

▶ Introduction of floating dredges helped to revive the mining industry in the Fairbanks area after World War I. As the giant, gravel-eating machines creep forward along river and stream valleys, buckets scoop up gravel and carry it to the top of a series of screens that sift out the gravel from the heavier gold. (Roy M. Corral)

to Fairbanks seeking work through the union halls, they returned to Fairbanks with their pockets full of money when their contracts ended. Second Avenue downtown became party central, lined with bars, prostitutes and drug dealers. Watching prostitutes solicit business became a regular hobby for downtown office workers. Crime started grabbing headlines.

Fairbanks also became a more expensive place to live. Businesses were accused of price gouging. Rents escalated. Property taxes soared. Retirees and people not employed on the pipeline had less to spend on increasingly expensive services and goods. Local stores and government found it impossible to compete with the pipeline for adult workers, and they turned to teenagers to fill vacancies. For a time, schools ran morning and afternoon sessions to handle overcrowding, and many students held full-time jobs opposite their class schedules, in some cases having work responsibilities and earnings almost equal that of their teachers. One teacher remarked that the students drove new cars while the teachers' lot was filled with clunkers.

The pipeline days became a historical

marker for the town. People talk about Fairbanks "before" or "after" the pipeline. Today, the pipeline passes close to the highway near Fox, its massive size dwarfing visitors who like to pose beside it for pictures.

In the meantime, a few gold mining companies and a small number of individuals have continued plugging away in the hills and valleys around Fairbanks. There may not be great numbers of miners anymore, but as gold mining goes, Fairbanks sees a goodly share of activity.

▲ *A floating dredge left behind a moonscape of tailings as it scoured the Chatanika Valley. (George Wuerthner)*

In 1993, the Fairbanks Mining District was the largest producing placer camp in the Eastern Interior Region, and much of the mining that goes on north of the Alaska Range depends on Fairbanks for supplies, services and transportation. The Fairbanks district has produced 25 percent of the gold mined in Alaska during the past 110 years.

That's why employment figures for the borough tell only part of the story. In 1993, the state Department of Revenue issued mining licenses to 110 individuals and companies with addresses in the Fairbanks borough who were gold mining. Yet nearly 280 mining licenses were issued for the larger Eastern Interior, Western and Northern mining regions, which Fairbanks serves. It's hard to get totals on the numbers of gold miners working in these regions. Sometimes, miners file the paperwork, but don't work their claim. Mining is highly seasonal, as well. The most recent estimate of the number of gold miners in the region is 883 for 1993. But estimates

range from 890 to as many as 1,500 gold miners. (In addition, the state's only commercial coal mine, Usibelli Coal Co. at Healy, about 120 miles south of Fairbanks, employs about 107 people.)

Seven of the 10 top gold producers in the state are based out of Fairbanks. The borough also gets its share of gold mining exploration and development dollars being spent on several dozen projects in the Interior. Among those, La Teko Resources, a Vancouver-based company, is exploring Ryan Lode on Ester Dome, 10 miles west of Fairbanks, and the True North prospect about 20 miles north of town near Pedro Dome.

The Ester Dome project is near the old gold-mining camp of Ester. The town sits in the middle of mining claims and is populated by an assortment of miners, artists and university professors. Ester started as a turn-of-the-century gold camp, then became the F.E. Co. operation headquarters for two dredges that worked Ester Creek from 1929 to 1963. The company moved some of the buildings from the community of Berry, according to locals. The new town was never formally platted, and property lines were drawn along the foot paths between buildings, the reason for the odd-shaped parcels of property in Ester today. Ester has its own mayor, town council, volunteer fire department, community hall, park, ice skating rink and local saloon, the Golden Eagle. The Ester Gold Camp hotel opens in summer to tourists.

Jewelry artist Judie Gumm and her husband Richard live in Ester in what used to be the dredge master's house. They've recently completed renovation of an old bunkhouse next door to use as a studio. Judie moved to Ester in 1973, soon after she came to Fairbanks from Denver at the urging of a girlfriend, who "didn't paint a pretty picture.... She talked about the cold and dark and ice fog.

"Fairbanks was just this outpost, but there was a sense of community. What appealed to me the most was you had to be a free thinker. You had to solve things for yourself, be responsible for yourself."

The Gumms, along with other folks in Ester today, are active in Common Ground, a local group working with several gold companies with claims on Ester Dome to resolve issues of water rights, noise abatement and reclamation.

Fairbanks also claims what will be the state's largest gold mine when it comes on line. Amax Gold Inc., through its subsidiary Fairbanks Gold Mining Inc., is developing the Fort Knox deposit, about 15 miles northeast of town. Construction starts in 1995 with production from the open-pit hardrock mine slated to begin in late 1996. Fort Knox's production is estimated to average 300,000 ounces annually for about 16 years. About 400 people will be employed during construction with about 250 miners employed at average wages of $44,000 a year, when production starts. Mining wages from Fort Knox alone will represent about a quarter of all non-government wages in the Fairbanks borough.

Mining's high wages are another part of the story ignored by employment statistics alone. Gold and silver miners statewide earned an average of about $4,715 a month in 1993. Oil and gas jobs paid the highest wages in the state, followed by heavy construction contractors, forestry, and metal and mineral mining. By comparison, retail jobs paid an average of $1,448 a month.

A similar comparison can be made for the Fairbanks borough, where gold miners earn about $3,461 a month. These wages are less than the statewide average for the industry, but still considerably higher than wages paid by retailers and service businesses.

All this, coupled with the fact that Fairbanks loves to celebrate its gold mining history, reinforces the image of Fairbanks as a gold mining town. Fairbanks sells itself as the Golden Heart City. Its annual Golden Days summer festival celebrates Felix Pedro's original strike. In winter, people root for the Gold Kings men's hockey team and in summer, cheer on the Alaska Goldpanners, a summer collegiate baseball team. For Fairbanks, gold mining is part history, romance, marketing savvy, lifestyle and even politics.

Fairbanks is home to the radical Alaskan Independence Party, (AIP) founded and led by the tough-talking, hell-raising and now deceased folk hero Joe Vogler, who was also a miner. Getting road access to mining claims was one of Vogler's passions. He once drove his caterpillar tractor across Yukon Charley Rivers National Preserve to his gold mine, in protest of federal restrictions. Vogler's party scored a coup in the 1990 general election, when Walter Hickel left the Republican party and signed on at the last minute as AIP's candidate and was elected governor. Hickel parted ways with the party soon after taking office, but Lt. Gov. Jack Coghill remained a loyal AIP member and ran for governor in 1994 against Republican Jim Campbell and Democrat Tony Knowles, who won. Coghill campaigned on such issues as building roads to mining claims and opening up more land for resource extraction. Most of his 13 percent of votes came from Fairbanks.

So is the image of Fairbanks the gold mining town a myth? Perhaps. But gold still has a hold on Fairbanks, as well as on many of the people who visit town. ■

▼ *Pipe is stacked in the Fairbanks Pipe Yard during construction of the trans-Alaska pipeline in the 1970s. The first oil passed through the pipeline in 1977; by 1993, more than 591 billion barrels of oil had traveled through the pipeline and through the terminal at Valdez. (Steve McCutcheon)*

Frozen Fantasy

▲ *The ice sculpting festival has been held at different locations in Fairbanks since its modern revival by the Chamber of Commerce in 1988. This scene shows the competition when it was held on the Chena River near the Cushman Street Bridge. The 1994 competition was held at Alaskaland. Organizers hope to hold the 1995 competition at their new site, to be called Ice Land, on the Chena across from Alaskaland. (Colleen Herning-Wickens)*

▶ *Blocks of ice for the Ice Art competition are cut from the ice-covered surface of a gravel pit off the Mitchell Expressway. The ice is light blue when cut, and Fairbanks ice has a good reputation among carvers. (Charles Newman)*

Ice carving was celebrated in Fairbanks as early as 1934, but the competition petered out until 1988 when the Chamber of Commerce bought ice in Seattle and revitalized the event. However, Fairbanksans took exception to purchasing ice Outside when a look around told them they had plenty of ice of their own.

In 1990, a private organization, Ice Alaska, took over the event from the chamber and now offers Ice Art, an international ice sculpting competition. When news of the quality of ice available in Fairbanks reached ice carvers, word of the event spread and sculptors began contacting Ice Alaska. Sculptors must submit an application verifying their credentials as sculptors and pay a $100 per competition entry fee. There are two competitions: the Single Block Classic and the Large Sculpture Classic. Prizes are awarded to the top five finishers in each of two categories, realistic and abstract. The single block event involves two-person teams that sculpt a block of ice 6 feet by 8 feet by the thickness of the ice, usually 3 feet to 4 feet. In the large block event, four-person teams get 12 blocks of ice 4 feet by 4 feet by the thickness of the ice. Teams assemble the blocks and create a scene.

Ice is becoming a popular sculpting medium in suitable habitats worldwide. Ice sculpting is now an event in the cultural Olympics held in conjunction with the sport Olympics. In the 1994 Winter Games in Lillihammer, Norway, Fairbanksan Steve Dean and his partner, Kevin Roscoe of Kirkland, Wash., won the bronze medal.

In 1995, the Single Block Classic will be held March 2-4; the Large Sculpture Classic takes place March 6-11.

— *Penny Rennick*

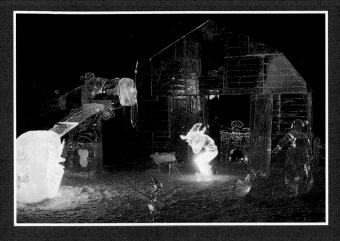

◀ The 1994 Ice Art competition produced this scene of a barn-stormer buzzing a farm yard, carved by a team from Michigan. The airplane has a 25-foot wingspan. (Harry M. Walker)

◀ A Fairbanks team sculpted this 10-foot-high Cinderella's slipper decorated with a pumpkin for the 1993 competition. (Steven Seiller)

▶ This sea horse was just one of several creatures adorning a 32-foot-high carousel carved by a California team. (Charles Newman)

▼ Dragons and sea monsters do battle in this sculpture entitled Sea King produced by a Pacific Northwest team of Lee Sheatle, Christopher Hussey, Jason Iwakami and K.G. Miyata. (Charles Newman)

▶ An abstract face stares at visitors to the Ice Art competition. The competition has two categories: abstract and realistic. Prizes are awarded to the top five finishers in each category. (Charles Newman)

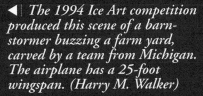

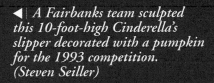

live year-round at the refurbished dredge, a National Historic Mechanical Engineering Landmark. Visitors can tour the dredge and several original bunkhouses, one of which serves as a restaurant, and pan for gold in front of the dredge where it stopped working. Most recently, Reeves bought F.E. Co.'s original machine shop in downtown Fairbanks, which he plans to restore eventually .

Fairbanks' other gold-mining attraction is the Little El Dorado Gold Camp, a working placer mine on the Elliott Highway that dates back to the early 1900s. Visitors board a narrow-gauge train for a two-hour narrated trip through mining history.

The claim was originally owned by the Swede Brothers, who did underground drift mining to reach placer gold deposits just above bedrock. They would dig vertical shafts, then tunnel out, or drift, along the paystreaks. They would tunnel during winter, stockpiling their diggings on the surface. In summer, they would work the stockpiled dirt through sluice boxes to recover the gold.

Visitors to Little El Dorado Gold Camp see early drift mining techniques reenacted at two of the original Swede Brother shafts. The train also passes through underground tunnels, where visitors see bones of prehistoric mammals preserved in the permafrost and exposed by the tunnel building. The train finally reaches a modern placer camp, oper-

The New Bonanza

About 40,000 of these visitors show up each summer at John and Ramona Reeves' gold mining camp outside town on the Steese Highway. The Reeves own Gold Dredge No. 8, a big floating gold factory, one of eight dredges that made up the F. E. Co. operation during the 1930s, '40s and '50s. The 1,065-ton No. 8 dredge and its crew of 80 worked one valley its entire career from 1928 until 1959. It dug 6,000 cubic yards of earth each

day, leaving a mountainous wake of tailings as it crept along.

Reeves, who dabbled in gold mining, bought the dredge in 1980 with the intent of restoring the derelict machine as a tourist attraction. At the time, it was almost hidden in a woods, where it had been abandoned after a short-lived tourist attempt in the 1970s by former owners. Vandals had stolen parts, used it for target practice and tried to burn it down.

Today, the Reeves and their five children

ated by colorful Fairbanks miners and AIP stalwarts Lynette and Dexter Clark. Lynette is also known as "Yukon Yonda," from her weekly talk show about mining on KFAR radio. Here, visitors gather around the Clark's sluice box for a quick lesson in placer mining before being turned loose to pan for gold.

Just as these gold-panning visitors like to look for color, Fairbanks likes to look for tourists. Tourism is emerging as Fairbanks' new bonanza. The numbers of tourists have increased each of the last five years, with more than 250,000 visitors to the Interior in 1993, spending an estimated $55 million in Fairbanks alone. Tourism has fed growth of the town's stores, hotels and other services in recent years.

Some of Fairbanks' visitors want to experience the gold-mining, river-boating history of Alaska's second largest city. Others visit town on their way in or out of state, stopping long enough to take in the University of Alaska Museum, the trans-Alaska pipeline and Alaskaland theme park, before traveling on by road or rail. Princess Tours, which dominates overland tour business in the state, brings thousands of visitors to town each year as part of larger swings through the north by

I ▶ *The Tanana Valley State Fair, held each August, gives vendors a chance to show off the vegetables and flowers grown under the 24-hour daylight of a Fairbanks summer. Nene Smith holds a bouquet of summer flowers, while behind her crafts people display hats and quilts. (Roy M. Corral)*

▲ *Singers and actors perform every summer evening at the Malemute Saloon, part of Ester Gold Camp, in "Service with a Smile," a variety show about gold mining history and featuring Robert Service poetry. The Ester Gold Camp, eight buildings listed on the National Register of Historical Places, is located on the main street of Ester, about 8.5 miles west of Fairbanks. (Roy M. Corral)*

train and bus. The company even built a new 200-room hotel in 1993.

The upswing in tourism has brought increasing numbers of independent travelers not connected to the big tours, said Carol Lay with the Fairbanks Convention and Visitors Bureau.

Also numerous smaller tour businesses operate out of Fairbanks. VanGo Custom Tours, for instance, offers personalized outings for small groups and individuals. These run the gamut and have included flying clients out to a dog musher's cabin for sled dog rides and dinner and visiting local artists in their studios, said owner Pat Walsh.

Fairbanks is also the launching point for visits to Interior Native villages and fish camps on area rivers. Arctic Village, an

Athabaskan community on the south slopes of the Brooks Range, operates tours out of Fairbanks. Closer in, the Athabaskan settlement of Stevens Village offers Yukon River Tours to take visitors by boat to a fish camp where they can stay the day or overnight. Here they visit with Athabaskan families fishing for and drying salmon, part of their summer subsistence culture. The camp also has a small museum, and the village plans to erect interpretative signs telling about the Athabaskans' role in the gold rush, how they helped the miners survive by showing them Native ways.

Most of Fairbanks' tourists arrive in summer, when the place is hot, green and bright with sunlight well past midnight. The Midnight Sun Run in June celebrates summer equinox, with nearly 21 hours of daylight. Participants, some in wacky costumes, line up for a 10 p.m. start. The long hours of daylight shine on other Fairbanks' specialties as well, such as the Yukon 800 Marathon Boat Race, a grueling two-day water race on three rivers from Fairbanks to Galena and back. And where else but Fairbanks can baseball fans enjoy America's pastime, played at night with no artificial lights. The Alaska Goldpanners, a team in the amateur summer collegiate league, plays throughout summer.

July in Fairbanks is full of festivals, with North Pole's July 4th celebration, the 10-day-long Golden Days commemoration of gold discovery, and the World Eskimo-Indian Olympics when Native athletes compete in traditional games and dances.

The waning days of summer are no less

▼ The $21 million Fairbanks Princess Hotel on the Chena River opened for year-round business in 1993. Princess Tours is one of the state's largest land tour operators and the Fairbanks Princess is one of three hotels recently built by the company. In late 1994 Princess announced plans to build a fourth hotel near Cordova in southcentral Alaska. (Fairbanks Princess Hotel)

▶ Claude Stover of Downey, Calif., gets a touch of the fever that propelled prospectors throughout the north about the turn of the century. Today, recreational gold panning is an important adjunct to the commercial mining that fuels part of the region's economy. (Roy M. Corral)

filled. August brings the Tanana Valley State Fair to Fairbanks, where giant 50-pound cabbages make for unusual photo opportunities. September brings one of the nation's hardiest marathons, the Equinox Marathon and Relay. It is a traditional marathon in distance from start to finish, 26 miles from campus to the top of Ester Dome, but not traditional in its vertical distance, a climb of nearly 3,000 feet. The race, first organized in 1963 to help preserve skiing and hiking

trails on university land, has been called "Fairbanks' fall sports classic" by historian Terrence Cole.

One of early winter's most anticipated events is the Athabaskan Old-Time Fiddling Festival. This three-day event showcases Indian and Eskimo musicians and dancers from along the Yukon River, playing fiddle tunes introduced long ago by gold miners and fur traders but since adapted to Native styling and language.

Then descends Fairbanks' cold and dark. Even so, winters here are increasingly popular. Fairbanks is becoming famous worldwide as a fine place to view northern lights. The Japanese, particularly, are enraptured with the aurora borealis, arriving in droves

During Golden Days, the Greater Fairbanks Chamber of Commerce sponsors the Rubber Duckie Race on the Chena River from the Illinois Street Bridge to the Cushman Street Bridge as entertainment and as a fundraiser. Each of the 5,000 ducks has a number on the bottom; the chamber sells $5 and $10 tickets for each number. The first 50 ducks to cross the finish line are collected in order of finish; in addition, a wild card duck is drawn. Winners vie for $20,000 worth of prizes and a good time in an event that can raise $75,000 gross for the chamber if all tickets are sold. At left spectators watch Carl Heimerman scoop some of the ducks; below a flotilla of bobbing duckies heads downstream on the Chena. (Both by Steven Seiller)

during the depth of Fairbanks' dark deep freeze. The town's hotels and tour operators drive skywatchers to good viewing spots when the lights come out. Chena Hot Springs, with its aurora-viewing chalet, caters to these celestial clients. They have a Japanese interpreter and the restaurant's menus are even printed in Japanese.

As winter gives way to longer, milder days, Fairbanks bustles with sled dog races, Native dance and art festivals, an international ice carving competition, even an annual international competition for the off-beat sport of curling, where teams of four slide stones across the ice toward a target. The Yukon Quest International Sled Dog Race from Fairbanks to Whitehorse, Yukon Territory, Canada, kicks off early spring fever, triggered by warming temperatures and returning sunlight.

Fairbanks' ice draws kudos from ice carvers, who come from all over the world to participate in the city's annual Ice Art competition. Carvers like the ice because it comes in large, crystal clear blocks that don't fracture easily. Kathleen Carlo, a renowned Athabaskan mask-maker and wood carver from Fairbanks, started carving ice a couple of years ago and eagerly anticipates each winter's competition. She says ice, under the blade of a sharp chisel, peels away like butter. "I love the transparency of ice and the way the light reflects through it. It's so different than wood, with different depths that you can look through to what's in back and in front. You get a lot of different dimensions."

The sculptures, illuminated by bright,

▶ Athabaskan fiddler and showman Bill Stevens plays dance tunes each November at the annual Athabaskan Old-Time Fiddling Festival in Fairbanks. The three-day party draws fiddlers and dancers from Indian villages along the Yukon River, where fur traders introduced the instruments and music nearly 100 years ago. Stevens was instrumental in founding the fiddle festival 13 years ago and continues to be a featured performer each year. (Roy M. Corral)

colorful lights, remain on display for about a month after the competition ends. An ice carving museum is in the works at the historic Lacey Street Theater, so summer visitors can see the frozen sculptures, displayed under colorful lights in refrigerated cubicles.

Tourism in Fairbanks, and much of Alaska for that matter, got its start after World War II with Fairbanks entrepreneur and bush pilot Charles West. In 1945, he got the idea of offering tours to villages along the arctic coast. He opened a travel agency and started flying sightseers from Fairbanks to Nome and Kotzebue, where they would take in Eskimo dancing and food. Most of his first passengers were construction workers from the military bases in Fairbanks. He started offering driving tours through town as well. All the while, he sold airline tickets to locals, booking cheap fares south on cargo planes that otherwise would have flown out empty.

West continued expanding his business, adding train and bus excursions between Fairbanks, Valdez and Seward, where clients

could board ships for their return to Seattle. Most clients for these tour packages came from Outside and enjoyed their stay despite relatively primitive conditions along the way, recalls West in his autobiography *Mr. Alaska* (1985).

In 1957, the business became Westours, a travel complex made up of motorcoach, cruise and sightseeing companies, and hotels. However in 1970, West teetered on bankruptcy and sold Westours to the Dutch cruise line conglomerate Holland America. West and his family later reentered the Alaska tourism market with another company, but

today Holland America and competitor Princess Tours, with its Grayline bus subsidiary, dominate Alaska's tourism market. Interestingly, they still offer the same basic sightseeing packages that West designed nearly 50 years ago.

Another of Fairbanks' early tourism pioneers, riverboat captain Jim Binkley, established a family business still going strong. Their *Discovery* riverboat cruises on the Chena River are an integral part of Fairbanks' summer scene.

Binkley's father, Charles, came across Chilkoot Pass at the turn of the century and

◀| *This aerial photo shows Fairbanks flooded by the Chena River in August 1967, the Chena's worst flood in recorded history. In 1979, the U.S. Army Corps of Engineers completed a flood control project with a 7.2-mile-long dam near North Pole, about 40 river miles above Fairbanks. When the river starts rising from melting snow or heavy rains, the dam's steel gates can be closed across the river to hold back flood waters. In 1992, the dam held back 6,000 surface acres of water that otherwise would have washed through Fairbanks. Normally, the gates remain open so boats and salmon can pass, and the impoundment area behind the dam remains dry. "We call it the big goose and moose pasture," says project manager John Schaake. Downstream from the dam, on some of the 20,000 acres of federal land designated for the project, is the borough's Chena Lake Recreation Area with parks, trails, campgrounds, beaches and a 250-acre lake stocked with fish. The recreation area is open year-round. (File photo, originally from Anchorage Museum, Photo no. B82.188.16)*

piloted boats on the Yukon, Susitna and Stikine rivers. Jim learned to drive stern-wheelers as a young man in Fairbanks, working the Yukon River at the end of the steamboat era. During World War II, he piloted military vessels on Alaska's rivers and coast. He returned to Fairbanks after the war, married and started a family. He and his wife, Mary, were going to school, working part time and running rivers in the summer when Charles West approached them in 1950.

West wanted Binkley to operate riverboat cruises for his tourists. Binkley took out a

$4,000 loan and bought a 25-passenger boat. In 1955, with business picking up, Binkley built the first *Discovery* sternwheeler in his backyard. Four years later, he lengthened the boat to carry more passengers. An even larger, 335-passenger *Discovery II* came on line in the 1970s.

By this time, the Binkley's four children were helping daily with the family's riverboat cruises.

In 1987, the Binkley's newest sternwheeler, *Discovery III*, reached Fairbanks, after cruising up the Yukon River on its maiden voyage.

The vessel was built in a Puget Sound ship-yard, then taken by barge to the mouth of the Yukon. The Binkley's story is contained in *Four Generations on the Yukon* (1988).

Today, the Binkley's sternwheeler plies the Chena River and a short stretch of the Tanana River. The four-hour trip becomes a short course in Alaskana, with narrations about the region's history, culture and geology. A bush pilot demonstrates takeoffs and landings on a riverbank as the boat cruises past. At Old Chena Village, a replica of an Athabaskan settlement that predates Fairbanks, passengers disembark for a tour with Native guides and long-distance sled dog musher Mary Shields trots out her team for the crowd.

Even without sailing the rivers, swirling pay dirt around a gold pan, or visiting Native villages, visitors can get a feel for those things at Alaskaland, 44 acres devoted to Fairbanks' history. Just inside the park's entrance sits the restored sternwheeler *Nenana*. In summer, visitors can tour the ship from engine room to pilot house. Mounted inside the ship is an elaborately detailed diorama of villages and settlements along the Tanana and Yukon rivers, where the *Nenana* steamed during the early 1900s.

From the *Nenana*, pathways lead to other pioneer theme attractions in Alaskaland. Gold Rush Town is composed of original pioneer log cabins turned tourist shops. The Palace Theater and Saloon show musicals and melodramas, while the Pioneer Museum offers a narrated exhibit of the gold rush. The park's Native Village has a museum of Athabaskan culture. A third museum is found at the Wickersham House, home of Judge Wickersham. Mining Valley features a working gold mining sluice box and the Alaska Salmon Bake, a popular dining spot where locals bring guests to taste salmon and halibut cooked over alder wood.

Although Alaskaland is geared to tourists, it also gets lots of local use. Admission is free, and families often bring their children to its

playgrounds, miniature golf course and musical carousel, throwing birthday parties in the covered pavilions. The park's Civic Center, a large round structure, serves as a year-round community center, with meeting rooms and exhibition halls. Its art gallery hosts traveling exhibits, and during summers the Northern Inua Show runs evenings in the center's theater.

Alaskaland was built on the banks of the Chena River in 1967 to celebrate Expo '67, the 100th anniversary of the Alaska purchase. The exposition opened just in time for the '67 flood, when the Chena River overran its banks. Plaques on an inside wall of the civic center and at park's train depot mark the highest water level. ∎

▼ *Increasing daylight in late winter and early spring brings out the cross-country skiers for the Citizen's Race. (Roy M. Corral)*

Songbirds in Plight - The Alaska Bird Observatory at Creamer's Field

By George Matz

Editor's note: *A frequent contributor to* Alaska Geographic®, *Matz is a consultant in the energy and environmental field.*

In midwinter Alaska's boreal forest is cold, dark and still. In early summer, this same forest is immersed in nearly 24 hours of daylight, the vegetation is bright green and the melodies of songbirds fill the air. These birds have migrated thousands of perilous miles to breed in the north.

When the first hints of fall appear, most songbirds seem to quietly slip away, leaving only resident species such as chickadees and redpolls to face the winter. Of the 77 species of songbirds that nest in Alaska, 66 migrate south for the winter. About one-third of these species fly as far south as Central and South America. These migrants

This mourning warbler, only the second record for Alaska, was caught in a mist net at Creamers Field. (Courtesy of Tom Pogson)

are called Neotropical birds, which includes species such as flycatchers, warblers, thrushes, swallows and some sparrows. Several other species of Alaska's landbirds, such as some raptor species, also migrate to the tropics for the winter.

The trip to warmer climes isn't exactly a vacation for a songbird. Many perish from storms, predators and other natural factors. More are killed by human-related factors such as windows and cats. Worst of all, when these birds arrive at their winter home, they may find that it is no longer there. Increased clear-cutting of tropical forests in recent years has eliminated large areas of songbird winter habitat.

In parts of North America, particularly the Northeast, nearly all Neotropical bird populations have declined sharply in recent years. Some scientists speculate that destruction of the birds' winter habitat may be causing their decline. But cause and effect is difficult to substantiate since scientists seldom know if the population of birds affected by the loss of habitat in Central or South America is the same population declining in some particular study area in North America. Also, besides natural mortality, fragmentation of breeding habitat throughout the Lower 48 and invasion of habitat by avian nest parasites, particularly the cowbird, also seem to be reducing populations of some species.

Better information will help resolve some of these uncertainties. For that reason, a growing number of ornithologists in North and South America, including Alaska, have started landbird banding projects during the past several years. Tom Pogson, executive director of the Alaska Bird Observatory (ABO) in Fairbanks, writes in the organization's Spring 1994 newsletter, *The Arctic Warbler*: "Mist netting and banding are essential tools in an ornithologist's bag of tricks because they allow us to simultaneously study important aspects of the ecology of small landbirds: species diversity, population levels, reproductive rates, the intensity and timing of migration, migration routes, habitat use, and more." Other tools are breeding bird surveys and nest monitoring.

Alaska is playing an important role in determining what factors are affecting populations of Neotropical birds. In terms of breeding grounds, Alaska is essentially a control case because, except for some coastal forests, Alaska's songbird habitats are mostly intact. Consequently, any population declines will probably be due to natural factors, such as weather, or problems on the migrants' wintering grounds. While these studies may not solve the riddle, at least they narrow the possibilities.

ABO Spreads Its Nets

In 1989, Tom Pogson, then a graduate student at the University of Alaska Fairbanks, began a songbird banding operation. Working for Alaska Biological Research Inc., Pogson set up a bird-banding station that year to study spring migration near Tok. Bird-banding requires special skills. In addition to having a masters degree in wildlife management, Pogson banded birds for several years before setting up the Tok operation. In summers 1977 and 1978, he worked with the late L. Richard "Dick" Mewaldt, a professor of zoology at San Jose State University who had established three renowned bird observatories in California: Point Reyes, South San Francisco Bay and Coyote Creek. In 1980, Pogson ran the bird-banding lab at Point Reyes. He says, "Dick is responsible for my interest in bird-banding, but I am only one of perhaps hundreds of banders that have received the gifts of his knowledge and enthusiasm for bird banding."

Once bird-banders have received sufficient training from someone with a permit, they can apply to the U.S. Fish and Wildlife Service (USFWS) for their own banding permit.

A yellow-rumped warbler is caught in a mist net. Bird-banding has five steps: First the bird is captured, then removed from the net, put in a cloth bag and brought to the field station. At the station a small band is placed around its leg. Next, identification and physical details of the bird are noted. Then the bird is released, often within minutes of capture. Although there is some mortality from mist-netting, if properly done, the mortality rate is less than 1 percent. (George Matz)

|▶ Rarely are hawks, such as this sharp-shinned, caught in mist nets. The nets are about 20 feet to 40 feet long and made of fine, black nylon or polyester mesh that flying birds seem unable to detect. The net's baggy pouches make for a soft landing. The nets are placed from the ground up to about 16 feet high in areas frequented by landbirds. (George Matz)

/▲ For the first time in 22 years, a Tennessee warbler was officially recorded for Fairbanks when this juvenile male was caught in 1992. (Courtesy of Tom Pogson)

Approval requires three credible references as well as demonstrated skills in handling captured birds. Tom received his master permit in 1981.

Upon completing the Tok project, Pogson knew that his future was "songbirds and what could be learned from systematic studies using mist nets to capture birds and banding to determine their movements and migration." He set about creating the Alaska Bird Observatory. Since national interest in Neotropical birds was heating up and Alaska was virtually a blank spot on the bird-banders' map, his timing was right.

In spring 1991, Pogson used his savings and support from

USFWS and Alaska Biological Research Inc. to get ABO off the ground. That year, he set up two mist nets in Fairbanks and a fall migration banding station near Dry Lake, at Mile 1376 of the Alaska Highway.

After the fall migration, Pogson had to shift his thinking from birds to administration. To encourage donations, ABO had to be organized as a private, non-profit corporation with tax-exempt status. Achieving such status can be a lengthy process. Instead, the Arctic Audubon Society in Fairbanks, which already had tax-exempt status, offered to take ABO under its wing.

During summer 1991, John Wright and John Schoen, Alaska Department of Fish and Game (ADF&G) biologists, convinced Pogson that the following year he should set up his bird-banding operation at the Creamer's Field Waterfowl Refuge in Fairbanks. ABO would be able to use some of ADF&G's facilities at the site, and the surrounding 1,800 acres of woods, wetlands and fields offered a good mixture of habitats for songbirds. Since this area was already used for nature education, having a banding station here would add to its visitor appeal. Also, the site's location in Fairbanks would allow greater volunteer participation than the more distant Dry Lake site. Since volunteers are an important resource in a low-budget operation such as a bird observatory, this was an important consideration.

In 1992, ABO moved its operations to Creamer's Field. It operated the banding station 42 days in spring, five days in summer and 45 days in fall. Using 35 mist nets, 783 birds were banded in spring, 65 in summer and 2,678 in fall. It turned out that 1992 had an unusually short breeding season with record cold and snow in May and September. Two birds rare to the Interior were captured: A Tennessee warbler was the first record in Fairbanks in 22 years; a mourning warbler was the second record for Alaska.

In addition to the Creamer's Field operation, ABO received a National Park Service contract to develop methods for monitoring landbird population trends in Alaska's national parks, cooperated with the Bureau of Land Management on a breeding bird survey along the Steese Highway, worked with USFWS on bird counts in the Fairbanks area and received a long-term contract from the U.S. Forest Service to report on Neotropical birds in decline that occur in Chugach and Tongass national forests. ABO became one of 19 non-governmental organizations and eight federal agencies involved with the Partners in Flight program, which is establishing a system for inventorying and monitoring North America's landbirds.

In its first full year of operation, ABO had revenues of $68,110 and expenses of $64,155. In 1993, ABO's revenues increased to $121,335, which paid for more equipment

Tom Pogson measures a bird, while intern Ana Marie Barber records the data. Measurements made during examination include the bird's weight and size of the wing, tail and bill. The fat level is then noted, as is its breeding condition, age (determined by examining the skull) and molt. For more advanced DNA and isotope studies, a drop of blood is extracted from the wing and a feather is removed. (George Matz)

and funded more projects. With two staff members, 11 interns and 35 volunteers, the number of birds banded in 1993 included 447 in spring (28 species), 66 in summer (11 species) and 1,723 in fall (29 species) for a total of 2,236. Pogson wrote in *The Arctic Warbler* that "There were striking differences in the capture patterns of birds during spring and fall migrations of 1992 and 1993." It appears that a smaller breeding population of warblers in 1993 resulted in less reproductive success. But similar to the previous year, "65 percent of the species and 78 percent of the individuals banded in '93 were Neotropical migrants."

Two banded birds were recovered in 1993. In August an

◀| *Sandhill cranes (red spots on head), Canada geese and pintails (white neck and belly) are just three of several species that use Creamer's Field. (Craig Brandt)*

|▶ *In 1994 the Alaska Bird Observatory began a project for the Alaska Department of Fish and Game on the olive-sided flycatcher, a species whose population seems to be declining. (James L. Davis, courtesy of Tom Pogson)*

alder flycatcher was recaptured that was banded in May in western Nebraska. A tree sparrow banded at Creamer's Field in September was apparently killed by a cat in October in Calgary, Alberta.

In 1994, twice as many birds were captured compared with 1993. New projects for 1994 included a study for ADF&G of the olive-sided flycatcher, whose population seems to be declining, and a project with

the Canadian Wildlife Service on use of DNA and geochemical analysis to pinpoint where birds summer and winter.

In addition to ABO, there were nine other landbird banding stations in Alaska and another in Whitehorse, Yukon Territory, by late 1994. The combined effort of these stations in 1994 banded 17,800 birds, of which 84 percent were Neotropical.

Three years of data from

ABO operations is barely enough to start drawing conclusions, but it can be said that there have been large differences in capture patterns from year to year, which may relate to natural factors. Also, Neotropical birds comprise a substantial portion of Alaska's songbirds. Any significant impact on the wintering grounds of these birds could impact populations in Alaska. Perhaps the most significant contribution of ABO and the other banding operations in Alaska is that there will finally be baseline data regarding not only Alaska's Neotropical migrants, but resident and other migrant landbirds as well. This data will help answer questions on the status of Alaska's bird populations.

Pogson concludes: "Birds are inseparable from their habitats. Because banding operations sample birds that wander throughout the Western Hemisphere, the capture rates of birds in mist nets are an indirect measure of environmental quality and change over large portions of the planet." Because of Pogson's efforts, it is less likely that the melodies of songbirds nesting in Alaska's boreal forests will become only a wistful memory.

Living in Fairbanks, A Cold, Crazy Place

Today the Chena River is a placid companion, tamed by a flood control project. Yet no one who lived in Fairbanks during the August 1967 flood has forgotten it.

Much like the pipeline construction, the '67 flood is a historical marker. People recall the devastation wrought as water spilled over the Chena's banks, covering almost all the town with up to six feet of muddy river. The only way around town was by boat. But just

▲ *Trees arched and broke with the weight of an early snowfall in September 1992. The storm caused power outtages for a week while crews worked throughout the greater Fairbanks area to repair broken lines caused by fallen trees. (Colleen Herning-Wickens)*

as keenly, they remember the outpouring of help townspeople gave each other, even while most of them were trying to cope with flood damage themselves. By the time the American Red Cross arrived on scene, the town was pretty well organized. Flood victims had flocked to College Hill, where campus became refugee central. People camped in dorms, halls, offices, even closets. The military performed rescue and relief flights, carrying whatever was needed wherever it was needed. Diapers and other personal necessities were distributed from a central collection point, sled dogs were rescued, a continuous barbecue was underway to feed the community.

Equally as remarkable was what happened with St. Joseph's Hospital. The 1908 building was in bad condition before the flood, yet voters had rejected bond proposals to fix it, including one on the ballot earlier in 1967. But after the flood, donations started pouring forth as people contributed to a grass-roots fundraising effort to build a new hospital.

"It's the people of Fairbanks that make it such a special place. We have extremes here. They rub against each other and cause all kinds of sparks, but then there are times when everyone works together," said Dr. William R. Wood. He should know, having served 13 years as president of the University of Alaska, and then a term as city mayor. He headed the hospital fund drive. Now at age 87, Wood is executive director of Festival Fairbanks, a nonprofit community service organization. Wood and his wife Dorothy Jane decided to stay in Fairbanks after he retired from the university in 1973.

"It's like no place we've ever found, and we've lived on every continent," Wood said. "It's an unusual product of the environment working on people, and the people working on the environment. The climate can be very harsh at times and very wonderful at other times.

"The people here are exceedingly independent. Many of them don't like the idea of governance and restraints, regulations and prohibitions. Yet they're equally as strong about wanting others to do the way they think things ought to be done.

"Something about the place makes people let go of their inhibitions to be their very natural best, or worst. If you can appreciate what you're into, you can relax and enjoy it. The combination makes it a delightful place to live."

Fairbanks does seem a place of extremes and contradictions. Taxes, for instance, get routinely routed in elections. The Interior Taxpayers Association formed about five years ago to work against further taxing. Yet most of the town depends on government jobs paid in some manner with tax dollars.

Fairbanks is the home of Alaska's environmental and conservation movement, of which residents Celia Hunter and Ginny Wood are matriarchs. They were civilian pilots attached to the military during World War II, who flew two planes to Fairbanks after the war in 1947. They made local news when Charles West interviewed them on his radio program on KFAR, and they ended up

▲ *Snow blankets these newspaper boxes along Chena Hot Springs Road, a 56-mile spur off the Steese Highway in Fairbanks that leads east to Chena Hot Springs. (Harry M. Walker)*

working for his fledgling travel agency, pioneering flightseeing tours to Kotzebue, among other things. A few years later, they were building a business of their own, Camp Denali wilderness retreat just outside the original boundaries of Mount McKinley National Park. They went on to organize the Alaska Conservation Society and Hunter later became the first woman president of

▼ *An expanding road system, including this new interchange near Geist Road and the Johansen Expressway, enables commuters to get around the sprawling city. (Roy M. Corral)*

The Wilderness Society. Both women became outspoken advocates of preserving special areas as wilderness and protecting Alaska from what they viewed as reckless development. Today, they live in Fairbanks at Dogpatch, a small community of like-minded souls north of the university. More recently, they've worked against proposed sales of large-scale timber tracts in the Tanana Valley, the main issue recently tackled by the local Northern Alaska Environmental Center.

Fairbanks is home to lots of people at the

other end of the spectrum, as well. Members of the Alaskan Independence Party are some of the most active and outspoken against land use restrictions, but there are others who promote mining, timber and development instead of the "lock it up" attitude they assign to conservationists.

"It's never dull here," asserts Ginny Wood. "I wouldn't leave no matter what. Take miners, they have a sense of place, a feel for the country — even though they muck it up. There's an addiction to the country, the land, the lifestyle that runs across a whole segment of people – environmentalists and developers.

"Everybody cares a lot about the land ...that's where you get your sense of place. Where else can you go out your back door, and ski 50 miles?"

As home to the state's university, Fairbanks has its share of liberal thinkers, yet the town has definite conservative leanings. Fundamentalist religion still plays a strong role in many people's lives. KJNP Radio broadcasts from a church community in North Pole. Personal freedoms are championed here, too. Ban the thought of gun control. The *Fairbanks Daily News-Miner* editorializes against it, and a borough assemblyman even introduced a resolution, which didn't pass, requiring residents to own guns. A curious change from Fairbanks' frontier days when observer John Clark remarked: "There were no gun fights, as I do not suppose one man in 500 carried a gun."

And then there's the matter of Fairbanks weather. Talk about extremes. But we'll get to that in a bit. First look more closely at what makes Fairbanks a modern contradiction.

The city itself straddles the winding Chena, just above its confluence with the wider, braided Tanana River. The downtown nestles into the south bank on a small bend of the Chena, its historic streets curving along the water.

Quaint log cabins and small frame buildings from pioneer Fairbanks still sit along some of the downtown streets, in the shadow of more modern high-rises. One of these, the steel-girdered Northward Building, was the setting for Edna Ferber's 1958 novel *Ice Palace*.

Today, Fairbanks has about 33,000 people, while the 7,361 square-mile Fairbanks North Star Borough has about 82,400. Some of the town's early pioneers, such as the Wien, Hutchison, Nordale, Hajdukovich, Schlotfeldt and Butrovich families, are still represented as well as some of the Natives who predated the pioneers. One of these is Howard Luke, an Athabaskan elder and one of the last survivors of Chena village. Fairbanks has a sizable Native community and gets a lot of traffic from Interior villages, as people come into town for medical care and shopping.

Downtown used to be the center of practically everything that happened in Fairbanks. Going to town on Saturdays meant going downtown. The grocery, the post office, the drugstore and the office supply store sat within a few blocks of each other and in making the rounds, you were sure to see familiar faces and people you knew, remembers photographer Roy M.

▲ *Native Alaska dancers show off their routines during the Quyana Alaska celebration. (Colleen Herning-Wickens)*

Corral who grew up in Fairbanks.

Then came the pipeline and changes. Hookers and bars took over Second Avenue, and newcomers filled the streets. A combination of congestion, crime and increasing city property tax rates made downtown businesses rethink their location, and they began moving out and into the more rural borough, beginning a sprawl of malls and shopping centers that continues today.

The newer roads through this sprawl keep their distance from the meandering river. Thoroughfares on each side of the water are joined by cross streets, interchanges and bridges in the grid of suburbia. One of the newest and shortest roads, the Johansen Expressway, runs only about three miles to reach practically the same destination as more circuitous routes.

In the latest commercial development that started in the early 1990s, national retailers moved to town, turning vacant farm fields west of downtown into parking lots and huge stores full of discounted clothing, plastic goods, hardware and groceries. Restaurants feature ethnic cuisine from around the world. Fairbanks is no longer an outpost where shelves are hard to stock. Daily cargo flights keep stores supplied with all sorts of luxuries.

Live Maine lobsters, New Zealand kiwi fruits, and the tropical flowering birds-of-paradise appear regularly in this far north city so distant from their origin.

All the while, downtown Fairbanks has had a hard time recovering. A new low came in 1989, when the swanky Seattle-based Nordstrom clothing and shoe store pulled out. Well-dressed picketers protested the loss of their favorite shopping spot. Nordstrom's old building, the original Northern Commercial Co. store, needed more repairs than

◄| *A hodgepodge of small shops reminiscent of small-town America front this view of stark, multistoried office buildings along Second Avenue. (George Wuerthner)*

the company wanted to make, its managers said. The building has since been torn down, replaced with a parking lot.

Meanwhile downtown is working to shake its image as a gathering place for drunks. Downtown merchants petitioned for walking police patrols during business hours. The city also assigned a patrolman to bicycle downtown during summer. Officer Hayden Bartholomew rides a 21-speed mountain bike down alleys patrol cars can't go, and has become a popular tourist attraction in his summer shorts uniform. Visitors flag him down to ask directions or advice on restaurants and to have him pose for pictures.

Golden Heart Park with its pioneer family statue, chiming clock tower and log cabin visitors center forms a riverfront centerpiece. J.C. Penney Co., which came to Fairbanks in 1966, still operates downtown, along with numerous art galleries and specialty shops.

Perhaps the most vibrant example of downtown revitalization is the busy Co-op Plaza. Formerly the Empress Theater, the building also housed a drugstore for many years. Today, the Plaza highlights an old-fashioned drugstore lunch counter in its center, in retro styling with vinyl booths, tile flooring, and thick ice cream milkshakes served in glass. Musicians play acoustical tunes during lunch on certain days. Specialty

shops, offices and the Musher's Museum encircle the restaurant, upstairs and down, with a second floor balcony overlooking the main floor.

The city itself is located in the geographic heart of Alaska, a place that residents often characterize as the "end of the line." Fairbanks is the last town of any size on Alaska's northern road system, passenger trains travel no farther north than here. It is surrounded by lots of wilderness and a few smaller settlements.

At the same time, Fairbanks is arguably the beginning, rather than end, of the line. The Steese and Elliott highways wind their way north to the Yukon River and ultimately Prudhoe Bay. It is the takeoff point for flights into the Interior, and it is one of the best places in the world for reaching space. While Fairbanks is often described as a pioneer outpost where people proudly flaunt their peculiarities and boast of woodsy acumen, it is also home to rocket scientists and computer wizards who not only travel, but help design, the global information highway.

Tour operator Pat Walsh defines the lure of Fairbanks as a place of "psychic room.... This place is not about the initial physical wow of visual impact," she says, "It's about frontier spirit, eccentricities, people making clear decisions about how they want to live. There's less social convention."

The Tanana Valley, with its waterfowl-rich wetlands and boreal forest of spruce, birch and aspen, fans south and west of town. To the north and east, the forest climbs into the knobby hills, which peak above tree line in caps of tundra known as domes. Some of them are well-known local landmarks popular with hikers and hunters, including Murphy Dome, Gilmore Dome and Ester Dome, which at 2,364 feet, is the highest point near town.

Scattered around Fairbanks are the communities of North Pole, Fox, Chena Hot Springs, Ester. The people who live here are a mix of conservatives, liberals, radicals, end-of-the-roaders, environmentalists, politicians, miners, professors, artists, authors, hunting guides, store clerks and dog mushers. Their ancestry spans the world, with people of German, English, Irish, French, Norwegian, Swedish, Scotch, Dutch, Italian and Polish descent, as well as Yup'ik and Inupiat Eskimo and Athabaskan Indian. Several years ago, a university linguist counted 74 different languages, not including the Native tongues, spoken on Fairbanks' streets.

To the south, the Tanana Valley buckles into the Alaska Range. These mountains on clear days are dominated by towering Mount McKinley. They insulate the valley and Fairbanks from weather off the Gulf of

▶ *Long a fixture in downtown Fairbanks, the Co-op Drugs lunch counter was renowned for its old-fashioned malts and milkshakes. Formerly located in the old Empress Theater, built in 1927, the drugstore opened in 1961. It closed in 1991, but the diner continues to operate in a portion of its former building that has been converted into a mall. (Roy M. Corral)*

Alaska to the south. Likewise, to the north, the Brooks Range stops coastal weather off the Arctic Ocean. With maritime climates slammed to a halt against these rocky block-

▼ *From their homes in the valley or on hills to the north, east and west, Fairbanksans look out onto an expansive boreal forest. (Colleen Herning-Wickens)*

ades, Fairbanks takes on its unique weather pattern.

The weather, even for Alaska, is extreme here. Hot summers that breed thunderstorms. Long days that grow giant vegetables and brilliantly colored flowers. And cold, cold winters with temperatures that routinely plunge below zero.

Because of its location between mountain ranges, air movement often is nil. Fairbanks suffers from air inversions three times worse than Los Angeles. Hot humid haze in summer hangs close to the land, as do winter's ice fogs.

Summer with its balmy 80-degree-plus days and 21 hours of sunlight is a welcome extreme, compared to winter.

The official record for cold in Fairbanks was minus 66, set in 1961. Temperatures of minus 40 and colder have lasted days at a time; nine days for the record. In those temperatures, tires freeze square on the bottom and go thump, thump, thump down the street. Motor oil solidifies. Metal cracks. Water particles in car fumes and wood stove exhausts freeze instantly, shrouding the city in a dense, gray, foul ice fog.

And there's the dark. The sun travels low across the horizon during its brief appearances each day in winter. The shortest day in December has only about four hours of sun.

Yet despite this, Fairbanks is an imminently livable city, according to a recent book that rates the best and worst small American cities. Fairbanks tied for fourth as the best place of 219 small cities to live, in the 1990 edition of *The Rating Guide to Life in America's Small Cities.* Fairbanks topped the list in what the author termed sophistication, economics and public safety, which included such things as the percentage of college graduates, number of TV and radio stations, voter turnout and number of residents born in other states. And it did well in the areas of diversion and recreational opportunities, education and transportation. It finished last in the category that measured proximity to major U.S. cities by road, measuring 2,265 miles from the nearest major league sports and art facilities in Seattle. Fairbanks is actually closer to a big city than the rating guide acknowledged. It is only 1,853 road miles to Edmonton in Alberta, Canada.

And, perhaps, not surprisingly, Fairbanks didn't fare so well in the guide's assessment of climate and environment. Summers there are fine, said the book, but the winters, well, left something to be desired.

But at least, winters in Fairbanks are dependable. Dependably cold, without thawing spells that turn feet of snow into midwinter slush, conditions typical of more southerly locales like Anchorage.

The people who call Fairbanks home don't seem to mind. Cliff Burglin, a 66-year-old veteran of Fairbanks winters, is one.

Burglin's parents met in Fairbanks during the gold rush, children of Austrian and

▶ *The disappearance of folk hero Joe Vogler, who was missing for more than a year before his body was found, prompted this display in a Fairbanks garden. (Harry M. Walker)*

German immigrants who moved to Alaska to acquire land and make a new life. Burglin and his wife, Joyce, operated the family's office supply store downtown for many years before he got involved in oil lease sales with his stepfather, geologist Bill Foran. "For a lot of years, I was that dummy from Fairbanks who filed on all the moose pastures on the North Slope. Then when the oil came in up there, I became that greedy speculator," Burglin says, chuckling. Today he manages the Bentley family trust, a former 800-acre dairy farm, 250 acres of which now holds a housing development and a shopping district that includes the Bentley Mall, Sam's Club warehouse and Fred Meyer.

"I wouldn't live any other place in the world," he claims. "There's a lot of us who feel that way. We sit around drinking coffee,

▼ *Border collie pups are curious about visitors at Dale and Marie Hoe-Raitto's kennel east of Fairbanks. (Colleen Herning-Wickens)*

▲ *Foreman Gary Murray (front), laborer Mark Rosser and backhoe operator Gary Barr position a new culvert for a driveway along the Goldstream Road Rehabilitation Project, designed to upgrade one of the feeder roads leading into Fairbanks. (Colleen Herning-Wickens)*

it's 50 below, our tires are flat, we can't get our cars started, and we still say we'd live here."

Dr. Wood likens deep winter in Fairbanks to being inside "a great cathedral, a great library" because of the quiet brought on by cold and dark. He admits that the lack of sun is something "you have to learn to cope with" and that means staying active.

As Celia Hunter puts it: "You have to like winter and you have to like outdoor winter or you don't like Fairbanks. If you don't ski or snow machine or whatever (outside), then winter can get pretty grim."

Skiing, like ice hockey, is a passion for many Fairbanks folks and a network of Nordic ski trails winds through the area. Karin Gillis, 33, a Swedish immigrant who skied competitively for UAF and more recently racked up a string of national championships in master's competitions, concentrates today on teaching and furthering the Junior Nordic ski program for Fairbanks youngsters. She says the cold isn't really a problem until temperatures drop to minus 40, although minus 10 is the cutoff for the Junior Nordic outings.

"There's something very special about the

▲ *Keeping up with the snow can be a full-time job in Fairbanks in winter. (Eric Rock)*

dark nights, the starry skies, the northern lights," Gillis says. "Summertime is beautiful, but I like the winters best." ∎

The Tanana Valley State Forest

By George Matz

Tanana Valley Forest Resources

Fairbanks lies in the heart of the Tanana Valley, a scenic trough flanking the Tanana River on the north side of the Alaska Range. Forested hills dip down to the river's northerly bank, and miles of flat muskeg and forest extend from its southerly bank to foothills of the Alaska Range.

The spruce/birch forest that carpets the lower elevations of the valley is one of the most biologically productive boreal forests in Alaska. Stands of towering white spruce occupy some of the warm, dry, south-facing hillsides and river bottoms that have been undisturbed for a century or more by fire, erosion or people. The

The Tanana Valley State Forest includes a number of areas that are conducive for tree growth. Here Ernie Whitney gets a close look at the largest quaking aspen in Alaska, which grows in the Cache Creek area of the forest. (George Matz)

younger hardwood forest is a patchwork of paper birch, quaking aspen and balsam poplar. On cold, wet permafrost soils, only stunted black spruce, tamarack and birch manage to survive. In addition to trees, the boreal forest is home for numerous shrubs, several of which produce delicious berries; herbaceous plants, many of which have healing powers; and mushrooms, some of which are valued by gourmets.

The mosaic of vegetation that typifies the boreal forest creates a diversity of habitat for wildlife. Moose browse on willow shrubs, caribou nibble on lichens, and bears (black and brown) feast on berries. Beaver swim in the sloughs, pine marten scamper through the black spruce muskeg, and other furbearers find a niche in the forest ecosystem. In addition, there are about 140 species of birds that nest in Alaska's boreal forest. These birds range from sandhill cranes to warblers. The forest also provides insects that salmon fry, grayling and white-fish thrive on. Northern pike, in turn, prey on these smaller fish.

Creating A State Forest

The abundance and diversity of forest resources in the Tanana Valley give area residents good opportunities for commerce, recreation and subsistence. To endow the public with opportunity to use these forest resources, the Alaska State Legislature in 1983 established the Tanana Valley State Forest (TVSF), the second state forest created in Alaska. Of the 29.1 million acres of forests and mountains included in the Tanana River basin, the state owns 14.8 million acres, of which 1.8 million were designated state forest. Although the land included in the TVSF amounts to only 6 percent of the total drainage area, approximately half (1.1 million acres) of the state-owned forest land in the Tanana Valley with commercial potential is within the state forest.

According to the enabling legislation, "the primary purpose in the establishment of state forests is the perpetuation of personal, commercial, and other beneficial uses of resources through multiple use management." Further policy is provided by Alaska's Constitution which states that, "replenishable resources belonging to the State shall be utilized, developed, and maintained on the sustained yield principle."

This mandate creates a challenge to the Division of Forestry (DOF), Alaska Department of Natural Resources (DNR), which is the lead agency for managing the TVSF. Users of the forest include not only loggers, but firewood burners, fishers, hunters, trappers, wildlife observers, outdoor recreationists, berry pickers, research scientists, miners, those who just enjoy the solitude that a visit to the forest bestows, and a variety of businesses that provide the goods and services often employed by all these forest users. While some of these activities may be compatible with each other, there have been conflicts between user groups, particularly over proposed large-scale timber harvesting.

Managing the Forest

Because the legislators anticipated conflict, the legislation creating the TVSF requires DNR to adopt a forest management plan and update it at least every five years. The first plan, completed in June 1988, states, "Because the plan is designed to promote multiple use, it establishes the rules or guidelines aimed at allowing various uses to occur with minimal conflict." DNR began review of the plan late in 1993. To solicit ideas from the public, meetings were held in spring 1994 in Fairbanks, Tok and Delta Junction. Proposed solutions were released in the fall, and a final plan is expected in spring 1995.

Concurrent with the forest management plan, the Division of Forestry is also completing its annual update of its "Five-Year Timber Harvest Schedule," another statutory requirement. This schedule, which is to comply with the rules and guidelines in the forest management plan, lists proposed timber sales, transportation access and reforestation efforts. The 1995 schedule leaves out the controversial large-scale timber sales that were originally proposed in the 1994 schedule.

This photo shows a recent clear-cut near the Cache Creek area. Some say clearcuts are an efficient method for logging and the disturbance they create is similar to a forest fire. Others disagree, stating that clearcuts waste other forest resources and are not at all like the patchwork effect of a forest fire. (George Matz)

Some of the issues voiced last year are likely to be heard again in discussing both the forest management plan and the five-year timber harvest schedule. Les Fortune, regional forester, thinks the most contentious issues that DOF needs to resolve are, "1) the type of timber harvest that occurs, particularly choosing between clear-cuts or selective cuts, 2) the size of harvest, and 3) developing road access for timber harvesting." He adds that, "There are very divergent views on these issues."

Larry Mayo, president of the Arctic Audubon Society in Fairbanks, says, "The most critical issue with the forest management plan is the retention factor." According to the 1988 plan, the retention factor is the percent of timberland that "will be harvested selectively or not harvested at all because of overriding non-timber resource values (that) may include fish and wildlife habitat and human use, recreation, private land, or cultural resources." The retention factors range from 10 percent for balsam poplar-white spruce forests to 1 percent for hardwood forests. Mayo says, "Such a low retention factor does not

provide adequate multiple-use management."

Sylvia Ward, executive director for the Northern Alaska Environmental Center, also wants changes in the new plan. She says, "It appears that the current forest management plan is designed for timber harvesting. Other uses of the forest, such as wildlife and recreation, are acknowledged but the plan does not ensure that these uses will be served as required by the enabling legislation for state forests."

On the other hand, Ron Ricketts, executive director of the Fairbanks Industrial Development Corp., says, "We have

an opportunity, because of the reductions in timber harvesting in the Pacific Northwest, for fairly significant forest industry development in Fairbanks. This can help the local tax base." He sees the next plan needing "a more expansive light than the first plan because of underutilized birch and aspen resources in the forest."

Ed Packee, an associate professor of forest management with the University of Alaska Fairbanks, says, "The objective of resource management is to insure productivity and biodiversity. We can lean on the ecosystem to produce benefits but we can't lean so

Fall foliage provides an ideal opportunity to observe the mosaic pattern of vegetation that typifies boreal forest. The dark green in this photograph of the Tanana Valley State Forest are stands of spruce, the light greens and yellows are hardwoods, mostly birch and aspen. (George Matz)

Fairbanks area residents have learned to make the most of the boreal forest that surrounds their homes. From firewood to commerical lumber to finely crafted wooden bowls, the spruce and hardwoods help support both a lifestyle and an economy. (George Wuerthner)

hard as to break it. We are nowhere near breaking it."

It may be too much to expect a plan to bring complete satisfaction to these divergent views, but a modest compromise could be achieved if forest products having high value-added potential were pursued. Examples mentioned by the DOF include paneling and furniture. This approach could result in more economic benefits to the Fairbanks area from fewer trees, which should please both developers and environmentalists. If so, the new TVSF forest management plan will have served its purpose.

Bibliography

Alaska's Great Interior. Vol. 7, No. 1. Anchorage: The Alaska Geographic Society, 1980.

Boswell, John C. *History of Alaskan Operations of United States Smelting, Refining and Mining Co.* Fairbanks: Mineral Industries Research Laboratory, 1979.

Brooks, Alfred H. *Blazing Alaska's Trails.* Fairbanks, University of Alaska Press, 1973.

Bundtzen, T.K., R.C. Swainbank, et. al. *Alaska's Mineral Industry 1993.* Special Report 48. Fairbanks: Division of Geological & Geophysical Surveys, 1994.

Cloe, John Haile. *Top Cover For America.* Anchorage: Anchorage Chapter, Air Force Association and Pictorial Histories Publishing Co., 1984.

Cole, Dermot. *Frank Barr: Bush Pilot in Alaska and the Yukon.* Seattle: Alaska Northwest Publishing Co., 1986.

Cole, Terrence. *Crooked Past: The History of a Frontier Mining Camp.* Fairbanks: University of Alaska Press, 1991.

—. *Ghosts of the Gold Rush, A Walking Tour of Fairbanks.* Revised and edited by Jane G. Haigh and Jon Nielson. Fairbanks: Tanana-Yukon Historical Society, 1987.

—. *The Cornerstone on College Hill.* Fairbanks: University of Alaska Press, 1994.

Dixon, Mim. *What Happened to Fairbanks.* Boulder Colo.: Westview Press, 1978.

Eielson Air Force Base. Edited by Public Affairs Office, Eielson Air Force Base. San Diego, Calif.: MARCOA Publishing Inc., 1994

Fairbanks Community Research Quarterly issues: Vol. XI, No. 3; Vol. XIII, Nos. 2&4, Vol. XIV, Nos. 2&3, Vol. XV, No. 2. Fairbanks: Fairbanks North Star Borough, 1988-1992.

Fairbanks Daily News-Miner. "Golden Days Edition". Fairbanks: *Fairbanks Daily News-Miner,* 1952.

Hays, Otis E, Jr. "White Star, Red Star," *The Alaska Journal.* Vol. 12, No. 3. Anchorage: Alaska Northwest Publishing Co., 1982.

Hulen, David. "Fairbanks Rates in 'Guide to Life'," *Anchorage Daily News.* April, 20, 1990.

—. "Funny Thing About Fairbanks at 40 Below," *Anchorage Daily News.* Jan. 29, 1989.

Hunt, William R. *North of 53.* New York: Macmillan Publishing Co., 1974.

Naske, Claus-M. and L.J. Rowinski. *Fairbanks, A Pictorial History.* Norfolk, VA: The Donning Co., 1981.

Pennel, Sgt. John M, edit. *Arctic Soldier.* Anchorage: Public Affairs Office, 6th Infantry Division (Light), Fort Richardson, Summer 1992.

Robb, Andrea. "Aboard the Nenana," *Heartland Magazine.* Fairbanks: *Fairbanks Daily News-Miner,* Oct. 9, 1994.

Robe, Cecil F. *The Penetration of an Alaskan Frontier, The Tanana Valley and Fairbanks.* Ph.D. dissertation. New Haven: Yale University, 1943.

Solka, Paul. "Adventures in Alaska Journalism." Fairbanks: *Fairbanks Daily News-Miner,* 1980.

Spring, Abe. "Early History of Tanana Valley." *Alaska-Yukon Magazine.* January 1909, pages 259-262.

Sturgis, Kent. *Four Generations on the Yukon.* Fairbanks: Epicenter Press, 1988.

The Army in Alaska. Fairbanks: Public Affairs Office, 6th Infantry Division (Light), Fort Wainwright, 1992.

West, Charles B. *Mr. Alaska, The Chuck West Story.* Seattle:Weslee Publishing, 1985.

Wickersham, James. *Old Yukon.* St. Paul: West Publishing Co., 1938.

Wold, Jo Anne. *Fairbanks: The $200 Million Gold Rush Town.* Fairbanks: Wold Press, 1971.

—. *This Old House.* Anchorage: Alaska Northwest Publishing Co., 1976.

The Newsletter
ALASKA GEOGRAPHIC.

*Requiem for IDITAROD
...see page 87*

KANATAK: *From Boomtown to Ghost Town*

◀ | *Russian Orthodox priests from Afognak and Kodiak islands ministered to Kanatak villagers around the turn of the century in a driftwood chapel. Later, villagers built this Russian Orthodox church, shown abandoned but still standing in 1978. No building occupies the site today. (Frederic H. Wilson/ USGS)*

▼ *Several old buildings still stood in Kanatak in the late 1970s, including this store and bar. Most of the buildings have since burned down. (Frederic H. Wilson/USGS)*

government's new school. Stores opened, and steamships called regularly with mail and freight. Then oil drilling ended. Kanatak shrank. The school closed, and the post office shut down in 1954. The village was soon abandoned.

Recently a regional Native corporation, Koniag Inc. of Kodiak, petitioned to acquire the historic Kanatak village property from the federal Bureau of Land Management, its current landlord. The village site is within the Becharof National Wildlife Refuge. At the same time, former Kanatak resident Marlane Shanigan, of Anchorage, is working with other

By L.J. Campbell

Only a few dozen people today remember Kanatak, an Aleut village on the upper east side of the Alaska Peninsula. Some rusty tools, old dishes and weathered boards litter the tall grass where the village once stood at the head of Portage Bay. The village was abandoned 40 years ago in an exodus so abrupt that guns, pictures, silverware and furniture were left behind; the buildings have since burned. Yet, for part of this century, Kanatak thrived as a Native village and oil exploration center and now it is getting renewed attention.

Kanatak, in its bayside landing off Shelikof Strait and a short mountain trail removed from Becharof Lake, was an important Native crossroads. Early villagers lived in sod barabaras, hunting and fishing in seasonal forays that often took them miles away. Visitors included Russian Orthodox priests, other Natives, fur traders and prospectors.

In the 1920s and '30s, Kanatak boomed as the nearest town to oil exploration on the peninsula. Outsiders poured in, bringing western clothes, conveniences and constructs. Villagers moved into wooden houses and sent their children to the

Kanatak experienced rapid growth in the early 1920s, with the arrival of oil prospectors. This 1924 overview shows the town spreading across the flatlands at the head of Portage Bay, with Kanatak Creek dividing the new and older sections of town. Supplies were lightered to shore from steamships anchored in the bay. (Anchorage Museum, Photo no. B65.18.178)

former village residents to re-establish the tribe of Kanatak, and they are contacting other former Kanatak villagers now scattered around Alaska and Outside.

Jeff Knauf, a fisherman in Kodiak, also has designs for Kanatak. Knauf wants to build a lodge for visitors and to house historical archives in Kanatak, on his property adjacent to the old village site. He thinks Kanatak's scenery and history will appeal to visitors eager to experience Alaska's wilder destinations.

Knauf first visited Kanatak by boat about 12 years ago, when he fished commercially in Shelikof Strait. The place entranced him. In the years since, he has returned many times, has collected about 300 Kanatak photos, poured through documents to chart its history, and, finally, bought one of the few privately owned parcels of land there. Sometimes relics from Kanatak – a coffee grinder, parts of a wagon, an old report card – turn up on his doorstep, left by people who've heard about his plans and want to send the items home.

| ■ |

Location largely made Kanatak. It sat at one end of an important trade route across the peninsula.

The village occupied flatland at the head of Portage Bay on Shelikof Strait, across from Kodiak Island. Early people could easily land or launch their small skin kayaks on the beach. Yet, Portage Bay's shallow waters were notoriously wicked during storms. Large vessels had to anchor out in the bay, and passengers and goods were lightered ashore. The village's first nurse and teacher wrote in 1923 that she was carried ashore on a man's back.

What distinguished Kanatak as a good village site was its nearness to Becharof Lake, a large inland body of water, rich in salmon and an important travel corridor. The lake's western end empties into Egegik River, which flows into Bristol Bay on the peninsula's Bering Sea side. A trail from Kanatak cut through a low mountain pass to Ruth Lake at the southeastern tip of Becharof Lake. The trail was the shortest overland route to Becharof from the Pacific Ocean side of the peninsula, and Portage Bay offered the closest landing to the trail.

Early Eskimos from the western Alaska Peninsula probably came this way to hunt and trade with Aleuts living along the peninsula's east coast and Kodiak Island. The route also was used early this century for mail, landed in Kanatak by steamers for transport to Egegik and villages on Bristol Bay. In winter, the mail went by dog sled across frozen Becharof Lake, down Egegik River, and north along the Bristol Bay coast to Naknek.

Also during modern times, Kanatak villagers traveled the route each summer, to work in Egegik's commercial salmon fishery and canneries.

Historic Kanatak dates back to the late 1800s. The 1890 census listed 26 Natives in seven families in two houses. Recent archeological investigations unearthed evidence of much earlier human occupation dating back 500 to 900 years.

Russian Orthodox priests from Kodiak Island mentioned Kanatak in their journals, written during trips along the Alaska Peninsula coast at the turn of the century. They referred to Kanatak as Kanatnoi, a village on Kanatnaya Bay.

Kanatak and a village on neighboring Wide Bay had been built by Aleuts fleeing unfair trading company agents at Ugashik, according to an 1893 priest's account. In 1902, priest Vassilli Martysh landed at the Kanatnaya Bay village where he found 23 people, all related, living in four barabaras. A Russian Orthodox chapel of driftwood served the villagers, who were led in psalm singing by a Russian-speaking Aleut named Ruff, wrote Martysh. The villagers trapped beavers and sold the pelts to the Americans at Kholodnaya (Cold or Puale) Bay, north of the village.

Also in 1902, oilmen arrived in Puale Bay. They drilled some wells, struck nothing, and by 1904 oil exploration ended. Soon after, Alaska was closed to mineral leasing. Meanwhile in Portage Bay, the small village of Kanatak was quietly growing. A few of the oil prospectors had stayed in the region as trappers.

Kanatak also became the new home for refugees from Katmai and Cape Douglas, coastal villages to the north destroyed in the 1912 Novarupta volcanic eruption. Dan

Amok, one of the Cape Douglas refugees, became Kanatak's Second Chief, a deputy to the chief. His daughter, Nida Nelson, was born in Kanatak in the 1930s and now lives in Anchorage.

Kanatak had felt shocks from the Katmai eruption of "such great magnitude that the barabaras, the Native's driftwood and sod huts, suffered heavy damage and many caved in completely," according to Wilson Erskine in *Katmai* (1962).

Erskine's father, Wilbur J. Erskine, was an influential Kodiak merchant who owned waterfront property in Kanatak. Wilbur Erskine was instrumental in Kanatak's 1922 oil boom.

Oil prospecting activity had revived in the region with passage in 1920 of a Congressional oil leasing bill. Wilbur Erskine and five other men from Kodiak actively prospected out of Kanatak in October 1920, filing 12 claims in the Becharof oil field, southwest of Mount Peulik. At this time, Kanatak had 69 people in 12 families.

Erskine's diary through 1921 mentions various people sailing to Kanatak for oil prospecting. Erskine and several others spent 11 days in the oil fields in July 1921, camping near a seepage on their Alaska Oil Co. claims, doing topographical and geological surveys.

In 1922, Standard Oil Co. started drilling 17 miles inland from Portage Bay. The SS *Redondo* arrived at Kanatak in August with the company's crew and drilling supplies, according to an article and diary excerpts in a 1926 Standard Oil Bulletin. It took 17 days to lighter everything to shore,

Dog teams pulling sleds laden with mail and supplies were a common sight on Kanatak streets during the early part of the century. In winter, the dog teams traveled across frozen Becharof Lake on their journeys between Kanatak and villages on Bristol Bay. (Kodiak Historical Society, Thelma Johnson Collection)

to Erskine's property across Kanatak Creek from the village. Erskine had invested in Standard Oil and was serving as the company's land agent in Alaska, according to Knauf, who

The arrival of prospectors brought better trails and eventually a territorial road from Kanatak leading inland to the oil fields. These folks gathered at the Dolff Smith Roadhouse for a picnic on July 4, 1923. The roadhouse was located on Becharof Lake, eight miles from Kanatak. The Alaska Road Commission worked on the road from 1924 to 1927, and continued funding maintenance and repairs through 1957. (Staff files, originally from the Anchorage Museum, Photo no. B65.18.175)

bought his Kanatak parcel from the Erskine family estate.

The crew spent six months building a wooden wagon road through mountains and swamps from Kanatak to the oil field. They used tractors, horses and dog teams to transport supplies from Kanatak. Drilling started on Standard Oil's "Lee No. 1" well in March 1923. Thick, tough sandstone and conglomerate slowed drilling to only inches a day and kept two men busy full-time, repairing drill bits and equipment, according to the Bulletin article. The oilmen put up with rain storms, raging winds that destroyed warehouses and sent a barn and horse sailing 40 feet, and winter blizzards that pinned them in their wooden buildings at the drill site.

Other companies working in the area included Associated Oil Co., which drilled Alaska Oil Co. claims. None of the wells produced. Standard Oil spent three years drilling Lee No. 1, reaching a depth of 5,043 feet only to have a "duster," oil field vernacular for a dry hole.

In the meantime, Kanatak underwent transformation. Within weeks of Standard Oil's arrival, the village population tripled to 200 people. The original village, on the flat east of Kanatak Creek, became known as "Old Town." The newcomers occupied "New" or "Company Town," a collection of tents, log cabins and frame buildings across the creek on the spit, near the old Russian Orthodox chapel, according to a 1994 Bureau of Indian Affairs report, written by Mathew O'Leary

as part of the proposed land transfer to Koniag Inc.

A post office opened in Charles Madsen's store. Madsen, a trader and coastal law enforcement officer, had briefly operated a store in Kodiak. When the oil boom hit Kanatak, he moved his family there, opening a restaurant and general store, renting out horses and buying furs. He stayed in business until 1924, then returned to Kodiak where he became a famous bear hunting guide.

During winter 1923, a fierce storm hit Kanatak. Winds destroyed several buildings and waves flooded town, carrying barges to land. But by year's end, Kanatak had recovered with 250 people and 73 buildings in Old Town, 59 buildings in New Town.

The village's school opened. Stella Fuller, a Red Cross nurse from Wisconsin, started teaching children and a few adults in an old saloon furnished with card tables. Some of the children took her fishing in their bidarkas, or skin kayaks.

In spring 1924, one of four U.S. Army biplanes engaged in an around-the-world flight made a forced landing near Kanatak. The oilmen received word over their wireless at the drilling site and sent a horseback rider to Kanatak to help search. Sailors off a nearby destroyer came ashore at the village for information, then towed the plane into Kanatak Lagoon, off Portage Bay, for repairs.

By September 1924, a small

schoolhouse was completed, with a bedroom and kitchen for a newly appointed government teacher. The teacher's initial report to the Bureau of Education was dour, describing the Native's barabaras as unventilated and "very unhealthy" and the town's drinking water source, Kanatak Creek, as "very impure."

The teacher continued, "No toilets have been provided and all refuse is thrown out around the doors. Also more than forty dogs are kept and five horses; all of which are around the houses. The fact that (villagers) are not at home in the summer months, and the climate is so cold with fierce winds, is the only reason they survive."

The 1924-25 school enrollment was 33 students, dropping to 20 the next year, mirroring the declining village population. The teacher reported, "The oil companies going out of this place, all of the people are leaving."

The boom had taken a toll in other ways. Teacher J.B. Henderson arrived in 1927 to take over the school and wrote a letter to the Bureau of Education telling of "many violations of the Prohibition Act" in Kanatak with sales of moonshine and whiskey to Natives and instances of public drunkenness. His four-page letter elaborated. Kanatak Aleut Chief Nicholai Ruff had sought to prohibit white bootlegger Bob Hall from entering the village, and Henderson had summoned federal agents after Chief Ruff and Second Chief Amok

set up a sting that netted a quart of whiskey. Henderson summoned federal agents from Kodiak. In a surprise raid that followed, the agent found 300 gallons of mash and arrested Hall and an accomplice, along with postmaster Margaret Rutschow and her husband William who were selling liquor from their store. Henderson praised the government's quick action: "All of this has had a very invigorating effect on the morals and morale of Kanatak....They understand that the flag of the United States does not float over this place for nothing."

Kanatak experienced something of a revival in 1938, when Standard Oil returned with two other companies to do some drilling in nearby Jute Bay. The town was considered large for the region, with a pool hall, store, bar, post office and church. Some of the Kanatak family names included Boskoffsky, Shanigan, Chernikoff, Amok, Taktak, Yagis, Kalmakoff, Pestrikoff, Ristofsoff, Knagin. The town census showed 134 residents in 1940, but drilling ceased that year. America's entry into World War II further drained the town as villagers enlisted, and by 1942 the town had only 81 people.

One of the few whites who lived there was Jack Lee, a trapper and mink farmer. In the early 1940s, Lee bought the remaining village store from Hilmer N. Evans, a merchant who had arrived during the oil boom. Lee also carried mail by dog sled on the Kanatak-Egegik route.

These Kanatak villagers took Red Cross nurse Stella Fuller fishing in their bidarka in 1923. One the back of the photograph, Fuller noted: "As we pulled in a cod, we hit it with a stick and laid it on the covered boat." (Courtesy of the Neville Public Museum of Brown County)

Lee was something of a gnarly character. He was known as "One-Eyed Jack," because he lost his eye in a fight, said Nida and Andrew Nelson in a 1990 interview, conducted by BIA's O'Leary.

Sometime in the late 1940s, Lee sold his store to Nick Shanigan, who moved his family into the building, said daughter Marlane. Lee left Kanatak and spent his last years in the Pioneers Home in Sitka.

One of Marlane's childhood memories is walking down the beach with her dad to a flashing navigation light, perhaps on Cape Kanatak, on the north side of Portage Bay. The federal government had installed an acetylene light at Cape Igvak on the bay's south entrance in 1931, at the request of Kanatak, Kodiak and Seward merchants and shipping company agents.

Kanatak's continued shrinking

and in the late 1940s, the school closed. The exodus of families accelerated. In April 1954, the village suffered a final blow: The post office closed. Most of the remaining villagers were away fishing and when they returned in the fall, they found little reason to stay. Without mail to move, steamers had stopped calling, leaving expensive charter boats or planes as the only way to get groceries.

People left Kanatak so quickly in those final weeks – perhaps hurrying

◄ | *Kanatak experienced a boom when oil companies arrived in the early 1920s and made the village their headquarters for drilling operations farther inland. This 1922 photograph shows oil field supplies being unloaded at Kanatak's beach. (Courtesy Chevron Library Services)*

▼ *Stella Fuller, far right, came to Kanatak in 1923 as a Red Cross nurse and began teaching school. Originally from Green Bay, Wis., she served the American Red Cross in Alaska for two years, including time in Kanatak. Shown here with her Kanatak students, she wrote, "I taught these children and several adults in our old saloon for a month. No books, no desks. We used card tables (with pockets) and card chips. Later got government to send in school and teacher." (Courtesy Neville Public Museum of Brown County)*

to get settled elsewhere before schools started, perhaps thinking they might come back – that they left most of their belongings and furniture. Some people did eventually return to reclaim some of their things, but most of the buildings were looted by fishermen and other people off boats.

Periodically, squatters occupied the abandoned buildings, including hippies during the 1960s, according to Knauf. Later, a reclusive Native moved in and appointed himself village keeper. Church officials found the man unwilling to part with the chapel's icons and old records. At one point he brandished a gun at law enforcement agents sent to retrieve the church's items.

Most of the buildings eventually burned in fires attributed to arson in the late 1970s and 1980s. The navigation light was removed from Cape Igvak in 1972.

In the past several years, federal agencies have conducted numerous site inspections and surveys in preparation to transfer the Kanatak village site to Koniag Inc. The regional corporation has no plans for the historic site at present, according to a spokesman.

Shanigan says that in talking with elders about possibly forming a Kanatak tribal corporation, she has found people wanting to return there to live. However, there are no Native allotments in Kanatak since villagers overlooked chances to file for land under the Alaska Native Claims Settlement Act.

Knauf, meanwhile, is slowly proceeding with plans to build a lodge. He recently had his land tested for possible environmental contamination, since it had been used as a staging camp by the oil companies. The work on his land was part of a larger assessment conducted in summer 1994 by federal inspectors as part of the land transfer to Koniag.

Knauf also plans to have an archeological survey of his property. "Having listened to the elders, it seems the respectful thing to do," he said. Everything about Kanatak intrigues him. At the least, he wants to build a place there for himself, his wife and children.

"Kanatak is just a wonderful place. Beautiful scenery, wildlife, tremendous history. Some sort of emotional tie keeps bringing me back. If I could go over there and live the rest of my life, that would be fine with me. People think I'm nuts, but this thing has been my dream."

Paul Boskoffsky

By L.J. Campbell

Kanatak holds many memories for Egegik salmon fisherman Paul Boskoffsky. He grew up in Kanatak and his family was one of the last to leave the village when it was abandoned in the mid-1950s.

Boskoffsky, 59, remembers trips from Kanatak to Egegik, where his family would fish and work in the canneries. Most of the villagers spent summers away, in Egegik, Chignik, Ugashik or Kodiak. A festive atmosphere would engulf the village each spring as families made preparations for the summer away. His family, other villagers and their dogs would walk along the trail through the mountains to Marraatuq, or Fish Village, a small year-round settlement at the edge of Becharof Lake. This would take about four hours. They kept boats at Fish Village. While there, they would go to Egg Island and gather gull eggs, some to take on to Egegik. They would also bury some eggs, a method of preserving them until they returned in the fall. Then they'd boat across the lake and down the river to Egegik.

When summer work in Egegik ended, they would boat back upriver with a winter's supply of flour, rice and other purchased groceries. They'd arrive at Fish Village in time for chum salmon, which they'd catch and dry for winter. They'd also pick berries and do a little hunting. Then they'd load everything in packs on their backs and on their dogs and walk home to Kanatak, often making several trips, said Boskoffsky.

Egegik fisherman Paul Boskoffsky assembled this montage showing five generations of Boskoffskys with ties to the village of Kanatak. Paul's father, Peter, (top right) was Kanatak's last postmaster. Paul's grandfather Nick Ruff (center) was born in the village in 1898 and served as Chief of Kanatak for many years. The gentleman at top left was Paul's great grandfather. Paul is shown at bottom left with his son Mark, also a fisherman in Egegik. (Courtesy of Paul Boskoffsky)

In the past decade, Boskoffsky has led young people from Egegik to Kanatak for Bible camp, retracing their ancestor's route. Once there, they poked around Kanatak's ruins, paid their respects at the old Russian Orthodox cemetery, and sat on driftwood logs along the beach. Driftwood washes ashore and ends up in great spiny walls lining the beach. When people lived at Kanatak, the ever-present driftwood provided building material, fuel and a place for the children to play. Boskoffsky said some of his most pleasant times as a child in Kanatak were spent down on the beach, playing myochi, a game similar to baseball, and making driftwood houses, boats and docks to play on.

Kanatak Chief Nicholai Ruff was Boskoffsky's maternal grandfather. "He was very pleasant, very influential because of his position," Boskoffsky recalls. "He worked hard. His lifestyle was a good example." Boskoffsky still has the uniform his grandfather wore as chief – a dark wool coat with military-style bars on the sleeve and a policeman's hat with "Chief of Kanatak" across the front. Ruff was born in Kanatak in 1898. He was active in the Russian Orthodox church and often dressed in his chief's uniform for special church occasions, Boskoffsky said.

Boskoffsky was born in 1935, the oldest of six children to Peter and Dora Ruff Boskoffsky. His dad had moved to Kanatak from Afognak Island. His parents conversed with the elders in fluent Aleut, but raised the children to speak English. Chief Nick Ruff could speak English, but preferred to talk to the children in Aleut, which they could understand but had trouble speaking.

Along with the chief, nine other men in the village were named Nick, recalls Boskoffsky with amusement. The Nicks went by numbers. His grandfather, of course, was Nick Number 1.

Boskoffsky also remembers store owner and trapper "One-Eyed Jack" Lee. Boskoffsky remembers one hot summer afternoon when he and his little brother walked into Lee's store.

at being a 19-year-old among 6-year-olds. He worked hard, advancing several grades a year, and finally graduated from Mount Edgecumbe in 1961, in the same class as younger brother Richard. The boys planned to surprise their father with an airplane ticket to Sitka so he could watch them graduate, but he died a month before commencement exercises. He was living in Egegik, where he was a fisherman.

Today, Paul fishes out of Egegik with his son, Mark, 22. Every few years, he visits Kanatak either by boat or foot or flies overhead. Even though the village is gone, he is reminded of what it used to be like.

Sometimes during salmon season at Egegik, when fishing boats clog Bristol Bay in a greedy frenzy, Boskoffsky says he thinks fondly back to Kanatak, how people hunted together and shared, less encumbered by worldly goods or desires. It's those times, he says, that his son who has visited there tells him, "I think it's time for us to go back to Kanatak."

Lee was napping, snoring rather vigorously. He wore false teeth and the teeth dropped off his gums and started bouncing around in his mouth. It so startled Paul's little brother than he ran out crying.

In 1949, Paul's mother fell ill with tuberculosis and went to the sanitarium in Seward. She was diagnosed with cancer while there. One day in 1951 the family was eating lunch at home in Kanatak, and they turned on their shortwave radio for the noon news. This was how they heard that their mother had died. "It was a real shock. None of us could eat," recalls Paul.

The Boskoffskys continued living in Kanatak until the village was almost completely empty, because Paul's father, Peter, was the postmaster. The fall after the post office closed, they moved to Seward, where his dad found longshoring work.

Paul had missed out completely

▲ *Members of a Bible Camp outing to Kanatak in the early 1980s found abandoned buildings such as Paul Boskoffsky's childhood home, which also held the Kanatak Post Office when his father, Peter, was postmaster. The wooden ribs of an old boat rest in the grass. (Paul Boskoffsky)*

▶ *Chief of Kanatak Nick Ruff (right) poses with his wife, Mary, (center), and daughter Dora outside a building in Kanatak. Dora later married Peter Boskoffsky. (Courtesy of Paul Boskoffsky)*

on schooling. He soon realized, as an illiterate teenager in the city, that he would have to learn to read and write. He beginning studying the alphabet in night classes. The next year he moved to Sitka, where his uncle arranged for him to start first grade at Mount Edgecumbe. Paul wanted an education so much that he shrugged off his embarrassment

Editor's note:
Former manager of the Iditarod National Historic Trail, Dean is a free-lance writer and natural resource consultant.

The pilot followed the old tram line north toward the Iditarod River. The helicopter banked and turned at the river, and through the windows we could see the ghost town of Iditarod: a few dilapidated buildings, a steam tractor and some rotting riverboats, all that's left of what was once the largest town in Alaska's Interior.

The helicopter landed, and we scrambled away with our packs. With cameras, tape measures and notebooks, our crew of historians and archaeologists from the U.S. Bureau of Land Management (BLM) and the Alaska Department of Natural Resources (DNR) set out to map and document the remains of the town. The two agencies are cooperating on a research project on the Iditarod National Historic Trail, and the first area of research is the history of the Iditarod Mining District.

The Northern Commercial Co. store looked ready to collapse in the first strong breeze. Horse collars, kegs of horseshoes and the remains of a double-decker wood stove sat on the ground outside the store. To the south, on the tundra, was the vault from the Miners and Merchants Bank. Nearby was the collapsed bathhouse, Iditarod's house of prostitution, and across the

Requiem for Iditarod

By Dean Littlepage

The west end of Flat, as it appeared in 1993, little resembles the town's heyday when prospectors poured into Iditarod country in 1910. Today, Flat's post office, at right, serves the one family that lives here year-round and miners who come in summer to work their claims. (Dean Littlepage)

the river was more than 500 miles, compared to 90 miles over the winter trail. The area of their find was so remote that it took more than a year for a major rush to develop.

river in tall grass and willows lay the 1910s sternwheeler *Prairie Belle*.

It was on June 1, 1910, that another riverboat, the *Tanana*, powered up the Iditarod with a load of freight and passengers headed for the mining district. The *Tanana* went as far up the river on high water as its draft would allow. On a muddy bank in a flat, treeless bog, the riverboat dropped its passengers. The spot became Iditarod City.

**Out of the Moss and (Tussocks)
Arose an Inland Empire**
—Masthead of the Iditarod Nugget *newspaper*

William Dikeman and John Beaton found gold on the Iditarod on Christmas Day, 1908, in their first prospect hole. In the spring they took their small sternwheeler to the commissioner's office in Ophir to record their claims; the trip on

---

The Iditarod River below Dykeman [sic] is a sluggish, deep, tea-colored, canallike stream and is, without a doubt, the crookedest river in Alaska. There are places where a steamer will travel five hours to make a distance that can be walked in 15 minutes by cutting across country.
—Anton Eide, Alaska Road Commission, 1910

People lived in tents in Iditarod the first summer, but by fall they had replaced the tents with wood frame buildings. In three months the *Tanana*'s passengers had built a small city with a platted, rectangular street pattern. Lining the streets were clothing stores, lumber yards and mining supply stores; the offices of lawyers, dentists and doctors; drugstores and jewelry stores, hotels and banks, saloons and cafes.

Iditarod was the legal and commercial center of the district, and the largest town. Flat, the town nearest the richest placer mines on Otter Creek, was connected to Iditarod by the old tram line; a Model T Ford on flange wheels ran gold and supplies over the wooden tracks.

Getting There and Away

Getting to Iditarod wasn't all that easy. In summer, boats made the long, winding trip up the Yukon, Innoko and Iditarod rivers to the town. The last stretch of river was often too shallow for deeper-draft boats. Dikeman, a short-lived town 85 river miles below Iditarod at the normal head of navigation, competed with Iditarod as the main river port for two years, but lost out and disappeared. A shallow-draft mosquito fleet – stern-wheeled, flat-bottomed boats that could run in two or three inches of water – took over the river during the low water of late summer.

In winter, the only way in or out was over the snow-covered Iditarod Trail between the city and the ice-free port at Seward. Dog teams carried mail, gold and passengers over the trail, but most people walked the 450 miles, staying at roadhouses along the way.

Life on the Iditarod

The social motto for Iditarod could have been "any excuse for a party;" the town was

This 1993 view shows Miss Tootsie's bathhouse, which stood at the north edge of Iditarod, north of the Northern Commercial store. (Dean Littlepage)

barely seven months old when the local Masonic Club put on Iditarod's first formal dance. Masquerade balls were the favorite party among the half a dozen social clubs in Iditarod and Flat. Prostitutes from the Row were welcome at the masquerade balls as long as they left before the midnight unmasking. The women of the Row even hosted an annual community party known as the pretzel dance.

On December 27, the Iditarod Masonic Club gave their first annual ball on St. John's Day. The ball was a grand affair. Everybody was in full evening attire and the ladies' gowns were beautiful. I wore a Paris gown of cream silk chiffon with a border of hand painted roses in pink, green and white.
—*Sarah Patchell in Iditarod, 1910*

Miners came from around the world to remote Iditarod. An account of the opening of the bar at the Discovery mining camp listed the nationalities represented: Scotch and Irish, Russians and Scandinavians, Italians and Greeks, Montenegrins, French and Belgians, Canadians and even a few Americans. Hudson Stuck, the

Iditarod's finest pose during the Arctic Brotherhood ball in the A.B. Hall in 1913. (Auringer Collection, Anchorage Museum of History and Art)

Episcopal missionary who raised the money for Iditarod's hospital, visited the mining camps to ask for donations. After a first-rate speech, he got no reaction from the crowd; only then did a foreman let him in on the joke — all the miners were from Montenegro, and not a one spoke English.

We aren't very good, because we have no church.
We aren't very bad, because we have no jail.
—*Motto of Flat in the 1930s*

There were no churches in Iditarod and Flat, and there was little crime and not much need for a jail. Sometimes men arrested in summer were stripped and left in a tent; the clouds of hungry mosquitoes guaranteed security.

One of the few crimes in the Iditarod District was the robbery of a gold shipment outside Flat in 1911. The two robbers got away with several heavy sacks of gold dust worth $35,000, but not for long; the boggy ground made their getaway slow, and one by one they abandoned the sacks on the tundra. A posse recovered most of the gold within a mile of where the robbery took place, only two hours after the crime.

Mushers tell of the capture at Tocotna of Angus Bronson and Louis Gorman, suspected of the big gold dust robbery on Flat creek late in the fall. The men were making a getaway via the Seward-Iditarod road when apprehended.
—Seward Weekly Gateway, *1911*

Supplies ran short during the long winters; happiness in Iditarod was the arrival of the cold storage barge in the spring. One year the town ran low on currency; another, the supply of pumpkin and apple pies was wiped out by Thanksgiving.

All last winter the inhabitants (of Iditarod) were without ingredients for the essential concoction of mixed drinks, such as lemons, sugar and spices. They had an abundance of ice, but were shy on other requisites.
—Seward Weekly Gateway, *1911*

But like in Alaska today, an up-to-date communication net linked Iditarod with the rest of the world. Within three months of its founding, the town had a telephone system, and by the second summer a wireless station made it possible to call anywhere in the United States or Canada from the Iditarod. Even the miners in the remote camps on Otter Creek were able to listen to the 1912 presidential election returns live on the wireless while they shot pool and toasted the candidates.

The End of the Line

The town of moss and tussocks peaked at about 1,200 people, with 3,000 in the district. After 1912, mining with dredges, which employed fewer miners, and the stampede to Ruby on the Yukon River began to rob Iditarod of its population. The "Guggs," the Guggenheim Syndicate, bought up most of the rich claims, and when the company moved its dredge to Malaya in 1918, most people left the Iditarod.

Many of Iditarod's businessmen left for the new railroad town at Anchorage. Z.J. Loussac, who owned Iditarod's City Drugstore, later became Anchorage's mayor. In 1930 the Miners and Merchants Bank moved to Flat, marking the end of Iditarod City. Flat still has five permanent residents and a handful of miners in summer.

Now even the river has deserted Iditarod City. The ghost town sits on an oxbow lake, the river having cut off the bend the gold rush town once was on.

Beginning in the early 1930s, the Iditarod River began cutting off this portion of its former channel, turning this stretch into a slough. Weathering away on its banks are the Northern Commercial Co. store and warehouse, center, and the remains of Day Navigation buildings across the slough. Day Navigation operated until World War II, getting supplies to Flat, which survived after Iditarod died as a town. Supplies were brought up the Iditarod River to the former town, then taken by road to Flat. Glen Day tried to keep the slough dredged out, but eventually had to build a road to a new landing on the Iditarod River farther from the old townsite. (Dean Littlepage)

Everybody Knew *Tootsie*

By Dean Littlepage

She is listed in the 1920 census as a 28-year-old laundress, but she was a lot more than that: local business owner, entertainer and mining claimant. Mattie Crosby was one of the first black women in the North, and one of its most successful early entrepreneurs.

Her bathhouse/brothel was on the Row at the edge of Iditarod, facing the street with its back to the river. From the ruins, it's not hard to imagine how luxurious it was: running water throughout, a carbide generator with lines to lamps of lavender glass in each room, thick straw mattresses on double beds, lace curtains and flowered wallpaper. Pieced together during several years, it was a maze of 14 rooms and more than 30 doorways; most of the rooms had buzzers she could use to call time on her customers.

Crosby, better known as Miss Tootsie, ran Iditarod's house of prostitution and a small roadhouse, worked mining claims throughout the area, and ran another bathhouse and a cafe in Flat after leaving Iditarod. She was born in Florida, daughter of a man from Bermuda and a woman from Virginia. Crosby came north to Dawson City with a white family from Maine that had adopted her after her mother died.

She lived in Alaska 72 years, not seeing another black for 30 of those years. At one remote mining camp where she stopped for dinner, a boy looked her over and told her that his family always washed up before eating. Crosby replied that no matter how much she scrubbed, her skin wouldn't change color.

Residents of Flat remembered her catered birthday and wedding parties, where she entertained guests with her singing and dancing. Penniless miners came to her for money and work; she took men who owed her money along to work her mining claims when she did assessment work in the fall.

The still that turned out a popular local whiskey was the engine for most of Crosby's profits. A federal agent, though, shut it down in 1924, taking Crosby for a six-month stay in the Fairbanks jail.

Crosby nearly drowned three times, and lost sight in one eye when she froze her face driving a dog team to Fairbanks. With her glass eye and a red wig on, "Miss Tootsie" was the Iditarod's unique and savvy businesswoman.

A friend to penniless miners, Mattie Crosby, known as Tootsie, was a pioneer businesswoman in Iditarod and later Flat, who would hire out-of-work miners to work on her mining claims. (Courtesy of Mark Kepler, Flat Library Association)

Editor's note: *Ed Darack is a professional outdoor photographer and writer based out of Davis, Calif. He is the author of* 6194 Denali Solo *(1995) about his solo ascent of Denali, North America's tallest peak, in 1991.*

The Hidden Giant

Story, photos and maps by Ed Darack

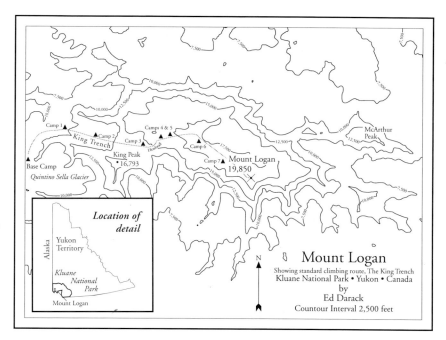

Mount Logan, the highest point in Canada and the second highest mountain in North America, is one of the greatest peaks on the globe. Hidden from view in most directions by the St. Elias Mountains, the 19,850-foot-high peak is visited by only a handful of people each year. Mount Logan lies is the heart of the Icefield Ranges of the St. Elias Mountains in Kluane National Park of southwestern Yukon Territory. Because of its location, Mount Logan is difficult to reach and quite an undertaking to climb. The only way to get to the mountain besides walking for weeks with cumbersome loads or dog sledding in, is to fly into the mountains in a bush plane. The St. Elias have been called the Himalayas of North America because of the many peaks exceeding 15,000, 16,000 and 17,000 feet, including Mount St. Elias at 18,008 feet and King Peak at 16,793 feet.

The peaks of this region are impressive in bulk as well as height. Mount Logan is arguably the largest massif in the world, measuring 25 miles long, 12.5 miles wide and more than 3 miles high. Lying only 80 miles from the Gulf of Alaska, precipitation is heavy. Precipitation in the form of snow and subsequent compaction and buildup of ice has formed the largest ice fields outside of Greenland and Antarctica. Mount Logan rises in the center of these ice fields.

An expedition to climb Mount Logan is a major undertaking. In June 1991, after successfully solo climbing Denali, I set my sights on Mount Logan. I soon realized that the logistics of the trip were far more complicated than at Denali. There are few detailed maps of the region and information on the peak is limited. After months of planning and research, however, I set out to climb Logan in June 1993 with my two climbing partners, Ryan Boyer and Aaron Martin.

After the drive up the Cassiar and Alaska highways, the three of us checked in with the mountaineering rangers at Haines Junction, Yukon Territory, and were granted final permission to go into the remote range. After one hour of driving farther west along the Alaska Highway, we came to the starting point of our climb, the Arctic Institute of North America's Kluane Lake research facility. From here, Andy Williams would fly us 100 miles into the mountains to the 9,600-foot level of Quintillo Sella Glacier at the western foot of Mount Logan. Andy runs a flight service and manages the research facility at Kluane Lake. We would be flown on-to the mountain in a Heliocourier, a single-engine, high-winged aircraft with short takeoff and landing capability. Our chosen route was the King Trench, a deep valley that ascends the western side of the mountain to the King Col. From the King Col the route ascends to the summit plateau and on to the top of the mountain.

Before our flight, the three of us separated our gear. Because we would have to be self-sufficient for up to five weeks, each of us would not only be carying a huge backpack, but would be pulling a heavy sled as well. Within our packs and sleds we carried three gallons of fuel each, stoves, food (spaghetti, energy bars, dehydrated cuisine, etc.), drink mix, ropes, climbing gear and camping equipment. For clothing, we wore polypropylene underwear, fleece pants and tops, and weatherproof outwear. For footwear, we used double-plastic, low-temperature mountaineering boots. Our hands were protected with thickly insulated mittens and our eyes with dark mountaineering glasses and goggles. Any exposed skin was thoroughly bathed in protective sunscreen. In addition to the mountaineering gear, I carried three Nikon camera bodies, two motor drives with two sets of spare batteries, a seven-pound tripod, six lenses, filters, maintenance equipment and 80 rolls of film.

Our flight in was spectacular. The morning was perfectly clear with stable winds. Andy would make two flights: one with myself and the bulk of the gear, and the second to transport the remaining gear and Aaron and Ryan. For the first flight, Andy took the door off the Heliocourier, and I strapped in to take aerial photographs of the expansive St. Elias Mountains. We flew over glaciers more than a hundred miles long and tens of miles wide. I worked furiously shooting photographs of the surrounding terrain that included formidable rock precipices, huge crevasses, cornices and a multitude of other alpine features. Once we landed, Andy and I quickly unloaded expedition gear and hauled it away from the aircraft while the engine idled. Andy took off and I set up camp and thought about the fact that I was likely the only person in the entire range at that time. When Ryan and Aaron arrived, we finished erecting our base camp and prepared for the next day's advance to Camp 1.

We began our climb at a slow rate. Each of us was hauling more than 110 pounds between our sleds and backpacks, and the altitude was affecting our strength. It took us five

When climbing mixed terrain (a mixture of rock, ice and sometimes snow), a climber must often climb over dry rock with ice climbing gear, a circumstance known in climbing vernacular as "dry tooling." Ryan Boyer climbs on a rock outcrop at 18,000 feet on Mount Logan with ice climbing gear.

stormy days and three camps to ascend to the King Col, at 15,000 feet above sea level. We camped just below the steep, 400-foot headwall that we would soon ascend to continue our climb. The night of our arrival, however, a huge storm moved in with 75 mph winds and new snow. Although we all felt strong, we welcomed the opportunity to rest in our tents for a few days, eat a lot of food and acclimatize. Three nights after the storm began, the sky suddenly cleared, and we quickly got on our way. Because the climbing ahead would be steep, sleds were out of the question. Thus we loaded our packs to full capacity. Because of avalanche danger, we ascended the headwall at 3 a.m. when snow conditions are most stable. The headwall proved grueling, and as we climbed steep snow and ice, our overloaded packs crushed us in the thin air.

Hampered by altitude sickness, frostbite and storms, our progress during the next few days was slow. Eleven days into the expedition, we reached the summit plateau at 17,500 feet. Although we had brought plenty of food, we had cached much of it. Running low, we had to begin rationing. Our plan was to acclimatize for two nights and then go for the summit, still miles away. Throughout the climb, I recorded the fantastic scenes found in this alpine area, my primary reason for coming to Logan. The evening we arrived at the summit plateau, I watched lenticular clouds form around one of Mount Logan's many summits. The scene quickly matured into one of the most beautiful atmospheric formations I have ever witnessed, as a giant, stacked wave cloud filled the sky. Although the rough conditions made us despair at times, scenes like these greatly helped to keep us going.

As beautiful as this wave cloud was, however, we knew that it spelled the arrival of yet another storm. For the next two days we camped in a total whiteout, endured

The lower reaches of some of the glaciers of the St. Elias Range often merge, as here with the South Arm and the Main Arm of Kaskawulsh Glacier.

temperatures as low as minus 40, and were pounded by 80 mph winds on the relatively unprotected summit plateau. Three days after arrival at our high camp, the weather broke and we made a dash for the top. After traversing a dangerous, avalanche-prone slope, we ascended a precarious jumble of crevasses and huge blocks of ice. At just more than 18,000 feet, I decided to camp, as I was totally exhausted, while Ryan and Aaron continued. The next day, suffering from frostbite on one of my toes and on my right hand's knuckles and totally out of food, I descended to 17,500 feet and waited for my two partners. Eight hours later, Ryan and Aaron staggered in, totally exhausted but happy as they had reached the summit. We endured one more

Climbers' tracks can be seen winding their way through Upper King Trench. Ed Darack, Ryan Boyer and Aaron Martin's camp below the headwall was located on this stretch.

brutal night of bitter temperatures, and woke moaning in pain because of the cold. Although the three of us were totally physically taxed, we moved quickly the following morning because all our food was gone and we needed to get down to our camp at the King Col where our sleds and supplies were located. It took 14 harrowing hours, but we finally made it. The most dramatic part of the descent was at the end where Aaron and I rappelled the headwall during the darkest part of the day. Ryan climbed down it, accidentally bashing his nose with his ice ax on the way, leaving a trail of blood down the slope. We camped that evening, relieved that the most dangerous part of the climb was behind us. The next day we made the long descent into

base camp, relaxed, called Andy on a portable, high-powered radio, and then camped. Because of thunderstorms back at Kluane Lake, we would not be able to get flown out until the next morning.

All of us cheered when we saw Andy's red Heliocourier streaking through the crystal clear, high mountain air and then landing. Andy made two flights, just as he had when he flew us in. Once back at Kluane Lake, we celebrated being back on safe ground and started to plan for the next big adventure.

INDEX

ALASKA GEOGRAPHIC® Back Issues

The North Slope, Vol. 1, No. 1. Out of print.

One Man's Wilderness, Vol. 1, No. 2. Out of print.

Admiralty...Island in Contention, Vol. 1, No. 3. $7.50.

Fisheries of the North Pacific, Vol. 1, No. 4.   Out of print.

Alaska-Yukon Wild Flowers Guide, Vol. 2, No. 1. Out of print.

Richard Harrington's Yukon, Vol. 2, No. 2. Out of print.

Prince William Sound, Vol. 2, No. 3. Out of print.

Yakutat: The Turbulent Crescent, Vol. 2, No. 4. Out of print.

Glacier Bay: Old Ice, New Land, Vol. 3, No. 1. Out of print.

The Land: Eye of the Storm, Vol. 3, No. 2. Out of print.

Richard Harrington's Antarctic, Vol. 3, No. 3. $12.95.

The Silver Years, Vol. 3, No. 4. $17.95.

Alaska's Volcanoes: Northern Link In the Ring of Fire, Vol. 4,
    No. 1. Out of print.

The Brooks Range, Vol. 4, No. 2. Out of print.

Kodiak: Island of Change, Vol. 4, No. 3. Out of print.

Wilderness Proposals, Vol. 4, No. 4. Out of print.

Cook Inlet Country, Vol. 5, No. 1. Out of print.

Southeast: Alaska's Panhandle, Vol. 5, No. 2. Out of print.

Bristol Bay Basin, Vol. 5, No. 3. Out of print.

Alaska Whales and Whaling, Vol. 5, No. 4. $19.95.

Yukon-Kuskokwim Delta, Vol. 6, No. 1. Out of print.

Aurora Borealis, Vol. 6, No. 2. $19.95.

Alaska's Native People, Vol. 6, No. 3. $24.95.

The Stikine River, Vol. 6, No. 4. $15.95.

Alaska's Great Interior, Vol. 7, No. 1. $17.95.

Photographic Geography of Alaska, Vol. 7, No. 2. Out of print.

The Aleutians, Vol. 7, No. 3. Out of print.

Klondike Lost, Vol. 7, No. 4. Out of print.

Wrangell-Saint Elias, Vol. 8, No. 1. Out of print.

Alaska Mammals, Vol. 8, No. 2. Out of print.

The Kotzebue Basin, Vol. 8, No. 3. Out of print.

Alaska National Interest Lands, Vol. 8, No. 4. $17.95.

Alaska's Glaciers, Vol. 9, No. 1. Revised 1993. $19.95.

Sitka and Its Ocean/Island World, Vol. 9, No. 2. Out of print.

Islands of the Seals: The Pribilofs, Vol. 9, No. 3. $15.95.

Alaska's Oil/Gas & Minerals Industry, Vol. 9,   No. 4. $15.95.

Adventure Roads North, Vol. 10, No. 1. $17.95.

Anchorage and the Cook Inlet Basin, Vol. 10, No. 2. $17.95.

Alaska's Salmon Fisheries, Vol. 10, No. 3. $15.95.

Up the Koyukuk, Vol. 10, No. 4. $17.95.

Nome: City of the Golden Beaches, Vol. 11, No. 1. $15.95.

Alaska's Farms and Gardens, Vol. 11, No. 2. $15.95.

Chilkat River Valley, Vol. 11, No. 3. $15.95.

Alaska Steam, Vol. 11, No. 4. $15.95.

Northwest Territories, Vol. 12, No. 1. $17.95.

Alaska's Forest Resources, Vol. 12, No. 2. $16.95.

Alaska Native Arts and Crafts, Vol. 12, No. 3. $19.95.

Our Arctic Year, Vol. 12, No. 4. $15.95.

Where Mountains Meet the Sea: Alaska's Gulf Coast, Vol. 13,
    No. 1. $17.95.

Backcountry Alaska, Vol. 13, No. 2. $17.95.

British Columbia's Coast, Vol. 13, No. 3. $17.95.

Lake Clark/Lake Iliamna Country, Vol. 13, No. 4. Out of print.

Dogs of the North, Vol. 14, No. 1. $17.95.

South/Southeast Alaska, Vol. 14, No. 2. Out of print.

Alaska's Seward Peninsula, Vol. 14, No. 3. $15.95.

The Upper Yukon Basin, Vol. 14, No. 4. $17.95.

Glacier Bay: Icy Wilderness, Vol. 15, No. 1. Out of print.

Dawson City, Vol. 15, No. 2. $15.95.

Denali, Vol. 15, No. 3. $16.95. Out of print.

The Kuskokwim River, Vol. 15, No. 4. $17.95.

Katmai Country, Vol. 16, No. 1. $17.95.

North Slope Now, Vol. 16, No. 2. $15.95.

The Tanana Basin, Vol. 16, No. 3. $17.95.

The Copper Trail, Vol. 16, No. 4. $17.95.

The Nushagak Basin, Vol. 17, No. 1. $17.95.

Juneau, Vol. 17, No. 2. Out of print.

The Middle Yukon River, Vol. 17, No. 3. $17.95.

The Lower Yukon River, Vol. 17, No. 4. $17.95.

Alaska's Weather, Vol. 18, No. 1. $17.95.

Alaska's Volcanoes, Vol. 18, No. 2. $17.95.

Admiralty Island: Fortress of the Bears, Vol. 18, No. 3. $17.95.

Unalaska/Dutch Harbor, Vol. 18, No. 4. $17.95.

Skagway: A Legacy of Gold, Vol. 19, No. 1. $18.95.

ALASKA: The Great Land, Vol. 19, No. 2. $18.95.

Kodiak, Vol. 19, No. 3. $18.95.

Alaska's Railroads, Vol. 19, No. 4. $18.95.

Prince William Sound, Vol. 20, No. 1. $18.95.

Southeast Alaska, Vol. 20, No. 2. $19.95.

Arctic National Wildlife Refuge, Vol. 20, No. 3. $18.95.

Alaska's Bears, Vol. 20, No. 4. $18.95.

The Alaska Peninsula, Vol. 21, No. 1. $19.95.

The Kenai Peninsula, Vol. 21, No. 2. $19.95.

People of Alaska, Vol. 21, No. 3. $19.95.

Prehistoric Alaska, Vol. 21, No. 4. $19.95.

Fairbanks, Vol. 22, No. 1. $19.95.

ALL PRICES SUBJECT TO CHANGE

Your $39 membership in The Alaska Geographic Society includes four subsequent issues of *ALASKA GEOGRAPHIC*®, the Society's official quarterly. Please add $10 per year for non-U.S. memberships.

Additional membership information and free catalog are available on request. Single *ALASKA GEOGRAPHIC*® back issues are also available. When ordering, please make payments in U.S. funds and add $2 postage/handling per copy for Book Rate; $4 each for Priority Mail. Inquire for non-U.S. postage rates. To order back issues send your check or money order or credit card information (including expiration date and daytime phone number) and volumes desired to:

The Alaska Geographic Society

P.O. Box 93370
Anchorage, AK 99509-3370
Phone (907) 562-0164; Fax (907) 562-0479

NEXT ISSUE: *The Aleutian Islands*, Vol. 22, No. 2. It was the first area of what is now Alaska to be invaded by Westerners and the last area to be invaded by Easterners. From the Russians who came more than 250 years ago to the Japanese who attacked 50 years ago to the modern commercial fishing fleets, the Aleutians have remained both a corridor and an outpost. This issue of *ALASKA GEOGRAPHIC*® takes a look at these distant shores. To members 1995, with index. Price $19.95.